A CATALOGUE OF

Angels

The Heavenly, the Fallen, and the Holy Ones Among Us

VINITA HAMPTON WRIGHT

PARACLETE PRESS
BREWSTER, MASSACHUSETTS

A Catalogue of Angels: The Heavenly, the Fallen, and the Holy Ones Among Us

2006 First Printing

ISBN 1-55725-421-4

Library of Congress Cataloging-in-Publication Data
Wright, Vinita Hampton, 1958-
  A catalogue of angels : the heavenly, the fallen, and the holy ones among us / Vinita Hampton Wright.
      p. cm.
  Includes bibliographical references and index.
  ISBN 1-55725-421-4 (alk. paper)
  1. Angels--Christianity. 2. Angels. I. Title.
  BT966.3W75 2006
  202'.15--dc22
                                                        2006015109
10 9 8 7 6 5 4 3 2 1

Published by Paraclete Press
Brewster, Massachusetts
www.paracletepress.com
Printed in the United States of America

To the beloved heavenly hosts,
who probably gain nothing from having books
dedicated to them.
Still I'd like to acknowledge their enduring presence,
holiness, and help.

CONTENTS

INTRODUCTION

PART ONE
ANGELS IN THE TRADITIONS OF ABRAHAM
1

PART TWO
A SHORT ENCYCLOPEDIA OF ANGELS
127

ANGEL PRAYERS
215

*T*his country has been in an angel craze for a few decades now. As with any popular trend, this one has been characterized by sensationalism and in some cases charlatanism, and of course rampant commercialization.

I've distanced myself from the angel craziness precisely because I really do believe in angels. I respect the reality of their existence too much to trivialize it. I believe that they are created and defined by God, and we must respect their existence while trying to learn what it means for us.

On a personal note, I am interested in the work and functions of angels, though I must confess that, to my knowledge, no angel has ever been manifest in my presence. That's not to say that angels have not been present, only that I have never perceived them. One or two people in my family have had experiences that seemed to involve angelic intervention. When my grandmother was a young woman and working in a city far from home, she had to take the train by herself one night, and a nice gentlemen was polite to her on the train, got off at her stop, and offered to walk her to her apartment. After they walked up the steps and she unlocked her door, she turned to say thank-you. But— yes, you've guessed it—no one was on the step with her. And from where she stood, with a clear view of the street, she saw no one departing down either side of it.

Grandmother forgot about that incident until I wrote a little book about angels years ago and sent her a copy. When I went home for a visit, she told me her story.

Years later, my husband was battling severe depression. He found a good therapist, but he was feeling so fragile at that time that he asked me to come along to his appointments. Dave, the therapist, agreed to this, and so I would accompany my husband and sit there silently during each session. I would listen, of course, but mainly I tried to pray. A good friend of mine suggested that I come up with an image that would represent God's care, or some other concept that would help me, and then meditate on that image during Jim's therapy sessions.

So at Jim's next appointment, I came up with something not very original. I imagined an angel standing behind my husband, hands clasped on Jim's shoulders while he talked with Dave. I sat there and closed my eyes and thought of this image; this was my prayer that evening.

In a little while, though, the image took on a life of its own. It was if my mind's eye had become a movie camera, and that camera abruptly backed up a few feet, and I saw that the angel was now standing behind my husband with arms raised, and with this angel, making a small circle around Jim, were four or five other angels, all with arms raised in petition for him.

Then, just as suddenly, the camera backed up again, much further, and what I saw made my heart pound and my throat catch. There were *circles and circles and circles of angels* surrounding my husband, concentric circles numbering hundreds, thousands of angels. And all of them had arms raised, sending prayers heavenward for him.

This vision was so overwhelming that my eyes flew open, and I began to cry silently, as the therapist and Jim continued to talk. When the session was ending, Dave said that I seemed to have been moved or upset by something. I related what had happened, and Dave, being very wise and himself a man of faith, said, "This is sacred, and I won't try to add anything by talking about it."

I still cannot tell or write this story without weeping. That image—and I remember how golden and shining it was—helped me through a season that was frightening and full of pain. On that evening, within a few seconds, I had been given a glimpse of God's love, manifested in this overwhelming support of the heavenly hosts who, invisible though they are, remain with us through every battle, arms raised to God's great heavenly presence.

My story is unique to me, but I am merely one of millions of people who experience the reality of angels at one time or another. There is so much raw data available on angelic works and encounters that the study of angels can become unwieldy. Not only that, but research about beings that remain, for the most part, unperceivable to humans lies beyond any empirical means of examination. Therefore, any study of angels needs a focal point from which the material can be organized. I decided to focus my attention on the three religious traditions that grew out of the faith of Abraham, patriarch of Judaism.

My own faith tradition is Christian, and my most immediate knowledge of angels comes out of standard Christian doctrine. Although Christianity is more than two thousand years old, it is rooted in the much older faith of Judaism. It is from the Jewish Scriptures and legends that so many of our beliefs about angels have developed. When the religion of Islam was born several centuries after Christianity, its prophet Mohammad claimed the Jewish, or Hebrew, Scriptures as part of his own heritage and thus established their importance within Islam. Islam's holy book, the Qur'an, offers its own versions of various sacred stories found in the Jewish texts as well as some from the Christian New Testament. Islam not only reveres the Jewish prophets but also considers Jesus Christ a prophet with a standing similar to that of Abraham or Moses.

During my twenties, I spent three years living and teaching in Jordan. I was able to tour a wide area, visiting Israel, Cyprus, Turkey, Syria, and Egypt. In those places I was deeply impressed by the various faces of worship toward God, the one God over the whole universe, the God of Abraham as recognized among Jews, Christians, and Muslims. I learned how frequently these three faiths merged in their worldview and even, to some extent, their theology.

Because these three major religions—Judaism, Christianity, and Islam—have in common the Jewish prophets and Scriptures, and because all three are staunchly monotheistic and have similar worldviews, I decided to turn to each of them for what they might tell me about angels. In doing so, I have attempted to gather information about angels that has survived the centuries. Although beliefs about angels existed in religions predating Judaism (and, in the cases of the Babylonian and Greek myths, exerted significant influence on Judaism), much of the lore that is most familiar to us was developed in these Abrahamic traditions. Consequently, most of our present-day beliefs about angels began with not only the holy books but also the legends and oral traditions given us by rabbis, Church Fathers and Mothers, and Sufi scholars and writers.

Much of what I will record is legend, because there is relatively little information about the heavenly hosts in the sacred scriptures of these three faiths. Most of what we know of angels has been passed down orally or has turned up in apocryphal and noncanonical sources. And though there are significant differences among these three major faiths, many of their beliefs about angels are very similar, and it is interesting to compare their stories.

This book is not a comprehensive study of angels and angel lore. I have tried to present information that is most accepted within a given tradition, which means that I left out the more obscure stories and theories. This book could be considered a primer on angels but certainly not a theological discourse on them.

Other books, such as those by Joan Wester Anderson, provide collections of the many contemporary stories of angelic encounters. That sort of book is inspiring in its own way, and I will leave the modern-day storytelling to others. But the stories you will find in *A Catalogue of Angels* are the ancient ones, the ones rooted in holy text that form our dreams and provide us with powerful symbols. These stories help us relate ourselves to a universe we will never understand yet in which we hold a position of great esteem, as ones who are loved by God and ministered to by God's many angels.

PART ONE
Angels IN THE
TRADITIONS OF ABRAHAM

There is an angel who watches over people, even in the dark.
This is Yode'a, the Angel of Losses. He watches lives unfold,
recording every detail before it fades. This angel has servants,
and his servants have servants. Each of the angels carries a
shovel, and they spend all their time digging, searching for
losses. For a great deal is lost in our lives.

—RABBI NACHMAN

It is certain that spirits have no bodily shape,
and yet scripture, in accommodation to us, describes them
under the form of winged Cherubim and Seraphim;
not without cause, to assure us that when occasion requires,
they will hasten to our aid with incredible swiftness, winging
their way to us with the speed of lightening.

—JOHN CALVIN

Angels include

the assembly of the Intelligences and Souls in the heavens;

yet their action is not confined to the celestial world.

They fulfill many functions in the daily religious life of man

as well as preserving the order of the cosmos.

It is ultimately the angels who guide man

to his final beatitude and who thereby

bring to fruition the purpose of creation.

—SEYYED HOSSEIN NASR

One
WHERE WE LEARN ABOUT ANGELS

There is a certain greatness in the angels; and such power,

that if the angels exert it to the full, it cannot be withstood.

And every man desireth the power of the angels, but their

righteousness every man loveth not.

—ST. AUGUSTINE

*A*ccording to *Webster's Dictionary,* Tenth edition, an **angel** is "a spiritual being superior to man in power and intelligence; also an attendant spirit or guardian." This definition has been boiled down from much lore and legend. We often think of angels as winged creatures with supernatural powers that assist us when we are in danger. Where did that image of wings come from? And why would these beings look out for our benefit if they are superior to us? How much contact is possible between humans and these creatures? These are just a few of the questions to be explored throughout this book.

For the purposes of this particular exploration, I define angels as spiritual beings created by God to carry out God's work in the universe and to aid humanity. They are spirit rather than material as we are; yet they are not the same as God. Neither are they to be confused with spirits of people who have died. They were created with specific characteristics and to perform specific functions. However, we have no way of knowing all of their traits or functions. We must confess, along with the earliest thinkers and philosophers, that the angelic world is for the most part beyond human comprehension. One difficulty in providing a clear definition of "angel" is that there are various nuances and differences in the definitions we find even within the faith traditions.

Another definition that becomes important in the study of angels is that of **demon**: "an evil spirit; a source or agent of evil, harm, distress, or ruin; an attendant power or spirit." Within the traditions of this study, a demon is generally believed to be an angel that fell out of God's favor through some act of rebellion or evil. In Jewish and Christian cosmology especially, demons and angels are closely related, because at one point they were both on the side of good and performed God's will. In the context of this book, "demon" lies within the angelic realm of spirits; a demon is in fact a fallen angel.

Two other terms that will appear a few times in the pages to come are **occult** and **magic**. Again, we turn first to the standard dictionary definitions. **Occult:** "not revealed, secret; matters regarded as involving the action or influence of supernatural or supernormal powers or some secret knowledge of them." Because angels are spirits and belong to realms that are outside the ordinary knowledge of humans, information about them has often been regarded as secret knowledge that humans could know only if revealed to them by a special messenger or by special means. Many legends about angels involve secret knowledge being given to certain humans so that they could understand more about the spiritual realm. This secret knowledge was supposedly passed down through the generations orally or was written in special books. The Hebrew, Christian, and Islamic scriptures—all given to human beings by God, what we refer to as "revelation"—contain information about angels.

Yet, often people have looked beyond the orthodox, sacred texts to other sources that claimed to contain secret knowledge of the heavens and heavenly beings. Through the centuries, certain individuals have become practitioners of secret knowledge, claiming to have the ability to communicate with spirits, whether angels, demons, or spirits of the dead. They also might seek supernatural powers, working through spells or incantations that they supposedly learned from spirits. In this way, occult practice would merge with **magic**, which is, according to Webster's, "the use of means (as charms or spells) believed to have supernatural power over natural forces; an extraordinary power or influence seemingly from a supernatural source." Generally, these practitioners have worked on the fringes of the orthodox faith communities. If not condemned altogether by religious authorities, they have been approached with care.

Angels, demons, occult, magic—depending on which sources we choose to study, these terms could take us in any number of directions. It's important to decide which sources to use and why.

The fact is, most of what we "know" of angels is legend. When we look at the sacred books of the three Abrahamic faiths, we find but a handful of angel names, the two constants being Michael and Gabriel. In other sources, however, I found more angel names than I could count, something I found puzzling, because the only angel names given in the Old Testament are Michael and Gabriel—and Raphael, if you're using the Catholic Old Testament, which includes the Book of Tobit.

So where did all these other names come from? And what about the angels I discovered that were linked to the zodiac, to the hours of the day, to the four directions, and so on? Where did information end and legend begin?

Four Tiers of Information

There are four general categories of information on angels, depending on your view of credibility and authority. For most "people of the book"—those whose faith is founded upon sacred scripture—the source of information on spiritual matters is quite important. And for all people of religious belief, a certain level of tradition and lore make up everyday belief and practice. This is especially true when it comes to the unseen world, with its heavens and angels.

Tier One

We start with what are considered the sacred scriptures of each faith. In Judaism this is the Tanakh, more commonly called the Hebrew Bible, which consists of Torah (books of Moses), Nevi'im (prophets), and Ketuvim (writings). Because the Hebrew Bible is nearly the same in content as the Christian Old Testament, to avoid confusion I will list the individual books here. Thus, the Tanakh consists of the following:

TORAH The Five Books of Moses	NEVI'IM The Prophets	KETUVIM The Writings
Genesis	Joshua	Psalms
Exodus	Judges	Proverbs
Leviticus	1 Samuel	Job
Numbers	2 Samuel	The Song of Songs
Deuteronomy	1 Kings	Ruth
	2 Kings	Lamentations
	Isaiah	Ecclesiastes
	Jeremiah	Esther
	Ezekiel	Daniel
	(minor prophets)	Ezra
	Hosea	Nehemiah
	Joel	1 Chronicles
	Amos	2 Chronicles
	Obadiah	
	Jonah	
	Micah	
	Nahum	
	Habakkuk	
	Zephaniah	
	Haggai	
	Zechariah	
	Malachi	

In Christianity, the Hebrew Bible is embraced as Scripture but renamed the Old Testament, then joined with the New Testament to form the Christian Bible. The New Testament consists of these books:

Matthew	Colossians	2 Peter
Mark	1 Thessalonians	1 John
Luke	2 Thessalonians	2 John
John	1 Timothy	3 John
Acts of the Apostles	2 Timothy	Jude
Romans	Titus	Revelation
1 Corinthians	Philemon	
2 Corinthians	Hebrews	
Galatians	James	
Ephesians	1 Peter	
Philippians		

The Catholic (and Anglican and Orthodox) branches of the Christian church accepted some writings as Scripture that were later rejected by the Protestants. These books are known as the Apocrypha and are added to the Old Testament:

Psalm 151	Azariah
Wisdom of Solomon	Epistle of Jeremiah
Susanna	Prayer of Manasseh
1 Maccabees	4 Ezra or 2 Esdras
2 Maccabees	Judith
3 Maccabees	Additions to the Book of Esther
4 Maccabees	1 Esdras
Sirach	
Baruch	
Tobit	
Bel and the Dragon	

Throughout this book, I will refer to texts primarily according to the names of individual books: the book of Genesis or of Tobit or of 1 Corinthians, rather than solely by "Old Testament," "Apocrypha" or "New Testament" because in many cases I will be discussing a passage that applies to both the Jewish and Christian communities.

In Islam, the Qur'an is the sacred text. Not only is the Qur'an sacred but also its very language—Arabic—is considered a primary component to the sacred character. To a devout Muslim, any translation of the Qur'an is not as viable as the Arabic Qur'an. The form of Arabic used in the Qur'an has become classical Arabic—understood by any literate Arab in any country of the world.

To say that these holy books are the sacred canon of their respective faiths does not mean that they are free of outside influences. For instance, Jesus refers to Beelzebub as the prince of demons in the Gospels of Matthew, Mark, and Luke. Most of us assume that he is naming the devil; we know, though, that Beelzebub was the name of a Syrian god that had, apparently, been absorbed into Jewish thought at the time, obviously not as a god but certainly as an entity. In the study of angels and demons, the lines between cultures and belief systems are crossed constantly.

Tier Two

The second tier of sources is comprised of the traditional teachings. In Judaism, the Talmud integrates the Torah with the oral tradition. Talmud essentially adds explanation of the Torah or, as one Jewish writer put it: "Torah says keep the Sabbath, Talmud tells how!" In fact, the essence of "Torah" is not just the sacred text but the many teachings about it, and this education, which is of utmost importance in Judaism, has been systematized for centuries to the effect that any self-respecting Jew would not attempt to simply pick up the Scriptures and absorb their meaning without instruction from another person (or at least a text by another person). It is nearly impossible to separate Scripture from the layers of rabbinical interpretation of the Scripture. In addition to this are the decades of tradition and various instructions about life, that come under the general term of Midrash. Not only were many of the beliefs about angels and demons generated from these teachings and traditions, but also some of the people we would consider to be the early angel experts were accomplished scholars of the Talmud.

For Christians—Catholic, Orthodox, and Anglican—church teaching forms much of the faith tradition. This includes not only official documents and decisions of the church but also its general history, including biographies and writings of saints and mystics. The nine choirs of the angelic hierarchy so standard to church teaching came out of the writings of Dionysius, whose identity is uncertain but whose claims were affirmed by Thomas Aquinas and other theologians.

In Islam, the Hadith are made up of the writings that concern all that the Prophet Mohammad said and did.

These writings include what God said through the prophet as well as what the prophet said himself. The Hadith concern all aspects of life, helping to form (along with the Qur'an) the basis for religious law. Although there are many references to angels in the Qur'an, the narratives about angels are often more elaborate in the Hadith.

Tier Three

Each of these three faiths has its mystical branch, and angels show up often in writings of the mystics. Numerous mystics and saints, of all three traditions, have had direct experience with angels. And in each of these traditions, some mystics have journeyed, in one way or another, to heaven and observed its structure and inhabitants.

Although mystics have often remained enigmatic to people in the mainstream, they have commanded respect in Jewish, Christian, and Muslim communities, and their explorations have done more to expand our view of angels than have the traditional theologies. In Islam, the Sufi scholars have been responsible for most of the study of angels. In Christianity, the mystics have dared to report their dreams and visions, which have kept alive our belief in angels long after science and technology disavowed them.

And the mysticism of Judaism has generated more material on angels than can be surveyed easily. Angels figure regularly in all three of its major mystical traditions—

Merkabah, Kabbalah, and Hasidim. Without the writings from Jewish mystics, the angel lore would be slim indeed.

Tier Four

This fourth level of angel information is complex, because the worldviews of the three faiths do not quite match up in regard to what is and is not acceptable as having merit and religious approval. Generally speaking, Tier Four involves sources of information that lie outside scripture, religious tradition and teaching, and mysticism. Because the fourth tier in Christianity is so well delineated, let's begin there.

Because devout Christians consider Scripture and church teaching to be paramount in authority, anything lying outside those two spheres is often suspect. And anything clearly forbidden in Scripture is taken, if not literally, then at least very seriously. So when the Bible forbids sorcery, divination, or astrology, each of which has involved interaction with angels and demons to some extent—the lines have been drawn clearly. From earliest times in Christendom, people who practiced sorcery, divination, and astrology were considered to be acting in opposition to God. Anyone who called upon, or conjured, angels or demons was in direct conflict with orthodoxy. Those who turned to the stars for help were also acting outside orthodox practice. Thus, "secret knowledge"— information about the spirit world that came from anything but Scripture and tradition—was by definition outside the bounds of approved practice. And so, within Christianity, a Tier Four source of information is prohibited and not sanctioned as a means of research.

Islam is almost as strict, but the mystical experiences of Sufism sometimes also entered the realm of magic. What might occur in the personal experience of a mystic could appear more magical than orthodox. For instance, what if a Sufi master, while in meditative trance, encountered an angel that took him on a journey and revealed to him specific information not covered by the Qur'an, the Hadith, or other Sufi experiences and writings? This would appear to fall within the realm of secret knowledge (occult); secret knowledge might enable a person to exercise power that other humans, in their relative ignorance, would not have, and superhuman powers are a form of magic. In this sense, the knowledge gained through this Sufi's experience would be mystical, but it could possibly go beyond mysticism and thus would fall within Tier Four. Yet a true Sufi practitioner was also by definition a devout Muslim, led by holy motives and always intent upon submitting himself to God's will. Most likely, Islamic authorities would not chastise the Sufi for his experience; at the same time, they would expect him to refrain from turning his experience into a divine revelation for all believers to follow.

In Judaism, the distinctions between faith and magic were blurred early on. Partly this was because to Jews scholarship and knowledge of the holy were highly revered. A practice that grew out of one's study of the Talmud bore merit in and of itself. From earliest times, knowledge of spiritual realms was considered the jurisdiction of the Talmudic scholars. Some of these scholars obtained knowledge that enabled them to communicate with angels (and, not as commonly, demons). As with Sufism, a Jewish mystic was planted firmly within the faith to begin with, and this assumed a certain level of wisdom and discretion. Out of respect for scholarship, religious authorities were hesitant to dismiss out of hand any practice that lay outside the mainstream. Joshua Trachtenberg throws some light on this in his *Jewish Magic and Superstition*:

> The Bible had pronounced an unqualified condemnation of sorcery. The Talmud, while maintaining this fundamental attitude, pursued its customary function of clarifying and classifying Jewish law, and so broke up the all-inclusive category of sorcery into several divisions, establishing varying degrees of guilt. Two main types of forbidden magic were distinguished: that which produces a discernible, material effect . . . and that which only creates the illusion of such an act or its effect . . .; or, as a further observation defined them, the one operates without the aid of demons, the other requires their assistance. The practitioner of the first type merits the Biblical penalty of death; the second is forbidden but not so punishable. Still a third kind of magic, "permitted from the start," involved the use of "the Laws of Creation," a term which was later interpreted to signify the mystical names of God and the angels.

The use of the names of angels constituted a wide-ranging practice within Judaism, from simple and superstitious folk magic to the more serious and powerful communication with both angels and demons. The rapid production of angel names in noncanonical writings was fueled largely by the many Jewish legends pertaining to their power. In Jewish traditions, to know the name of a spirit was to exercise significant power over it. If a person were to learn the name of an angel or a demon, he could call it forth—or, conjure it—and it had no choice but to come. One of the most famous legends has King Solomon conjuring a demon and demanding to know the names of the other demons who were persecuting the temple workers, as well as the names of the angels who had power over those specific demons.

And so, inevitably, in each tradition the discussion of angels sometimes merges with the discussion of magic and superstition. This is true in all three faiths, but the volumes of angelic/magical material in Judaism can be attributed to the fact that it is the oldest of the three. Rabbinic teaching did not condone magical practice, just as the Church Fathers forbade it in Christianity; yet Jews and Christians alike succumbed to superstition and were at times tempted to look for supernatural means to deal with life's hardships. This was particularly true during the Middle Ages, when magical thinking ran amok and so many people sought magic spells and charms to exert some sort of control over their circumstances.

In any religion there are fringe movements—this is as true today as it was centuries ago. In any religion there are groups of people who claim secret knowledge that is unattainable by most other people. Sometimes fringe movements involve interaction with the entities of the spirit world, whether angels, demons, or spirits of the departed dead. Devout Jews, Christians, and Muslims are usually wary of such interaction, and their leaders often warn against the dangers of seeking supernatural power that does not issue from prayer and personal holiness.

In searching the Internet or the typical bookstore for material on angels, you are much more likely to stumble upon non-traditional material than on traditional. That is, I would categorize much of this material as Tier Four. For instance, there are a number of popular books and well-developed Web sites that claim to help you communicate with your angel guide or that provide a hodgepodge of information with little or no reference to sources. Thus you might read about the Archangel Gabriel on the same site that offers ritual prayers for conjuring him.

But in the mainstream of the Abrahamic faiths, angels are God's servants, not ours, and good angels are obedient to God, whereas fallen or evil angels (demons) are those who try to grab glory for themselves, who do not obey God, and who are antagonistic toward God's creation. They do not exist so that we can conjure them to do our bidding or to help us succeed in our endeavors. They are by no means on the same level as God, and, although we may include angels in our prayers—in the same way we include the saints or our departed loved ones—they are not the focus of our prayers or other devotions. Thus, in researching this book, I have relied chiefly on the sacred scriptures and on the traditions (more accurately, on authorities on the traditions), avoiding almost all occult sources while acknowledging some of the better-known occult sources in the Encyclopedia.

A Brief Description of Sources

For sacred stories and texts in the Jewish tradition, I have used the Tanakh—the Jewish Scriptures as translated and published by the Jewish Publication Society. For stories and texts from the Christian tradition, I have used the Catholic Bible, New Revised Standard Version. I used Mohammad Picktall's English translation of the Qur'an for the sacred text of Islam, although I know that any English translation is a far cry from the Arabic text, in both literary form and spiritual power.

Once you move beyond the sacred scriptures of these three faiths, and the traditional teachings about them, material about angels is found in several categories of literature.

Apocryphal texts are those that were ultimately rejected for inclusion in a collection of sacred Scriptures. There are various reasons for exclusion—heretical doctrine and questionable authorship being the main two—but not all apocryphal books were considered such all the time and by all groups. Thus, we have several books in the Catholic

Bible that were excluded from both the Hebrew Bible and the Protestant Bible. The one book of this set that has had the most impact on our belief in angels is the Old Testament book of Tobit, which gives us a warm, human story about the angel Raphael.

There are numerous apocryphal "acts" and "gospels," and some of them have references to angels. For instance, the Gospels of both Bartholomew and Nicodemus describe in detail Jesus' descent into hell after he was crucified and before he was resurrected; Bartholomew especially describes angels and demons. The Gospel of Peter gives a specific account of angels descending and ascending at the Resurrection and assisting Christ out of the grave.

A **pseudepigraphical** text is a work that is attributed to a historical figure—in the case of Judaism, a work done under the name of a patriarch. Several of these works have contributed significantly to angel lore, such as the books of Enoch, the Ascension of Isaiah, and the Testament of Solomon.

One important subset of the apocryphal and pseudepigraphical writings is the apocalyptic literature. We have visions of the end of time ascribed to everyone from Abraham to Peter. Apocalyptic literature includes some combination of the following: end times and the destruction of the world, the final struggle between good and evil, the last judgment, and the establishment of God's kingdom. The very nature of apocalyptic writings guarantees that angels, demons, and heavenly realms will be involved.

Here are just a few examples of some apocryphal and pseudepigraphical works that have contributed to angel lore:

Ascension of Isaiah: This book (more likely two different works) describes Isaiah's battles with the devil, and his ultimate martyrdom. And it gives us a detailed description of Isaiah's journey through the seven heavens and his subsequent discussions with angels in those heavens.

Apocalypse of Paul: claims the apostle Paul as its author and describes his extensive tour of heaven and numerous conversations with angels.

Book of Jubilees: talks of the angel Michael's explaining to Moses aspects of the Book of Genesis; also explains how angels assisted people on earth.

Books of Enoch, 1–3: Written at different times and by different authors, these writings give accounts of Enoch's vision of heaven. 2 Enoch, also called The Book of Secrets of Enoch, gives an account of the fall of Satan and his angels; it also describes Enoch's journeys through the seven heavens and his encounter with God and the angels.

Gospel of Bartholomew: gives an account of Jesus' descent into hell following the crucifixion and contains much information that is forced from Satan about the realms of angels and demons.

The War of the Sons of Light Against the Sons of Darkness: from the Dead Sea Scrolls, gives intricate instructions for battling against the "sons of darkness, the army of Belial."

Testament of Solomon: This claims King Solomon as its author, and is an early primer on demonology, naming many demons as well as the angels who have power over them.

Why even acknowledge sources whose origins are questionable and which have never been accepted within an orthodox faith tradition? These writings are important because, even though they did not become part of sacred canon, they did influence belief within the traditions. For instance, the Jewish belief that the patriarchs became angels upon entering heaven goes directly to the chronicles of Enoch, in which the man who "walked with God and was no more" went to heaven and was transformed. Our most common concepts of heaven have developed from accounts of journeys through the celestial realms and into the presence of God and the angels. So although we know that the books of Enoch were in fact written by various authors at different times and even in different regions, something about their message has rung true for centuries, and it has become part of our collective vision about heaven and its inhabitants.

I have attempted to sort out for readers what beliefs have been more enduring within the traditions. I have tried to point out when the material consists less of doctrine and more of legend or is even occult in origin. Many contemporary sources on angels do not make such distinctions, probably because the lines are so blurry. To people who believe that all the beliefs are mere mythology anyway, such distinctions are not important. And to people who believe everything, including the latest angel "dictation" available at the bookstore, there is little need to explore the hows or whys of any distinct religious tradition.

To a lot of people who believe in angels, however, it's important to understand what the great prophets and believers have passed along to us. The history of a belief means something, and the meaning of a term could make a real difference in how that term is applied. For those readers, I hope to have done the subject justice. The study of angels can be daunting. But the stories we find are full of wonder, beauty, and hope.

Two
ANGELS IN JUDAISM

In that hour God replied to them: "Abraham, My friend, Isaac,
My chosen one, and Jacob, My firstborn, I cannot now save them
from their exile." Then the angel Michael, the Prince of Israel,
wept in a loud voice, "Why, O Lord, do You stand aloof?"
—from a legend about the Exile,
Tree of Souls: The Mythology of Judaism

*I*n a lengthy section on angelology in Jewish Encyclopedia.com, the authors confess that "It is impossible [when discussing angels] . . . to fix the boundaries between the speculations of scholars and popular notions, between individual and general views, between transient and permanent ideas." When one sets out to study angels in the Jewish tradition, this statement is confirmed again and again. Outside of the information found in the Hebrew Scriptures, beliefs about angels and systems to describe them abound in rabbinic teachings, in the writings of Jewish mystics, and in numerous non-canonical works. In the Christian tradition, the Catholic Church settled on one hierarchy of the heavenly hosts; but in Judaism there are several, depending on whether the source is the Talmud, the Kabbalah, or several options in between.

Jewish belief about angels did not emerge as an original set of ideas but grew and developed over time. The Israelites' religion was shaped as the nation traveled through, dwelt with, and was dominated by, other nations and cultures. Of particular influence upon the Jewish understanding of angels were the Babylonian and Persian systems of belief because of Israel's extended periods of exile under those peoples. For instance, the Jewish hierarchy of angel realms is quite similar to that of a Persian court. And a few angel names seem to have been adapted from entities in these earlier pantheons of gods and spirits.

Within Judaism itself, angelology was dominated first of all by an early group that was either Essene or Hasidic. Writings in the Dead Sea Scrolls, such as *The War of the Sons of Light Against the Sons of Darkness,* give prominence to angels, their names, and the means by which a mortal could conjure these spiritual forces and use them. Such teaching involved elaborate ritual and demanded strict righteousness on the part of the mortals. Some of these teachings evolved into various noncanonical works, such as writings under the name of Enoch.

Jewish mysticism, in the form of Kabbalah, further developed philosophy and belief about heavenly realms and their inhabitants. The most prominent kabbalistic text is the Zohar, or "book of splendor," which ranks the orders of angels and gives instruction for how to talk with them. Some kabbalists carried angelology into magical practice that included naming scores of angels, developing rituals for conjuring them as well as practices for exorcising demons.

In Judaic literature there was much historical precedence for the magical use of knowledge about angels and demons. Two early texts that revealed secrets of the spirit world were the *Book of Raziel* and the *Testament of Solomon*. The *Book of Raziel,* reportedly given to Adam (or Noah, depending on the legend) by the angel Raziel, revealed much secret knowledge about the spirit world and was passed along through the generations. And the *Testament of Solomon,* according to legend, is King Solomon's account of events that happened during the building of the Temple. Solomon's foreman was plagued by a demon, and Solomon asked God's help, whereupon Michael the angel brought to Solomon a magic ring. Not only was Solomon able to control the demon through this power, but also he was able to call up many other demons and extract important information from them, such as where they came from, what they did, which angels had power over them, and what specific words or phrases could be used to exorcise them. Scholars estimate that the *Testament of Solomon* was written in the second or third century. They place the *Book of Raziel* at about the eleventh century. These sorts of writings were not necessarily Jewish in origin; a number of them have a clear stamp of Christianity, making specific mention of the twelve apostles or of the virgin who gave birth to the messiah.

The Middle Ages were a heyday for angelology and demonology. Legends and writings attributed everything that happened to some spirit, for good or evil. At that time, magic was as believable an explanation for what happened in the world as anything else. Thus, angels and demons were connected with hours of the day, days of the week, months of the zodiac, physical elements of the world, the four directions, and on and on. Jewish mysticism took hold of all this, as did Medieval Christianity. We owe a lot of our current angel lore to the imaginations of those believers, whether Jew or Christian, who sought to make sense of the world at a time when there was little science to provide explanations for events, whether catastrophic epidemics or daily problems and heartaches. Angel lore has long been linked with astrology; the same impulse that caused people to read the stars for spiritual fulfillment moved them to create a universe filled with spirit beings who sent plagues or brought rain, who moved the planets and aided or hindered childbirth.

Jewish mysticism of thirteenth-century Germany gave us Eleazar of Worms, a kabbalist who wrote *Book of the Angels,* a major text on the subject that continued to influence the way people thought of heavenly realms and how they influenced life on earth.

Judaism is filled with legends about angels, and it's difficult to tell which legends are "mainstream" and which are more connected to magical or occult sources. There is one legend that God was displeased with people's invoking the powers of angels, so he changed the angels' roles, thus putting the whole system into confusion. The Talmud does not condone magic or sorcery—and does not mention the conjuring of angels. But in general, the Jewish faith does not make the same kinds of distinctions between canonical and noncanonical writings as we find in the Christian community. Whereas most Christians see a significant difference between their Bible and the various writings that were not accepted into the canon, Jewish scholars have had a more elastic approach to legends and theories, regarding them not as sources to be proven false or true but simply as components of the larger story that is the communal faith experience.

The Jewish approach is so elastic, in fact, that the rabbis seemed to have worked with angel themes in great earnest at times. They had a penchant for reading between the lines, often inserting angels in Scripture narrative where none had been mentioned. And so in Jewish lore we find several angels helping or hindering Abraham, or Noah, or Moses, or helping David fling the rock that felled Goliath. One legend tells us that God sent two angels to be guardians to Adam and Eve in the Garden, but when the angels left to say their prayers in God's presence, that's when the serpent sneaked in and tempted Eve. In the enhanced version of Esther's story, from the Hebrew book of Esther, there's an angel manipulating every circumstance imaginable.

At times it has appeared that the Jewish teachers and scholars used angels in stories more as teaching devices than as real characters. Perhaps an angel enters the picture and argues with God about what he's about to do. The angel asks, why? And God answers. In this way, the rabbis used this construct to tell a story while making an ethical or philosophical point.

And sometimes a Jewish writer could use an angel to solve a theological problem. In one legend we learn that whenever God has to make a pronouncement of judgment—of some action taken by God, or allowed by God, in order to punish evil—God doesn't make the pronouncement; the angel Gallizur does. This is because, at least in the mind of whoever created this legend, God is good and cannot make evil pronouncements. So an angel is appointed for that distasteful job.

What we find, then, is that stories about angels have served various purposes, similar to the way mythology works. They explain how evil entered the world, or why God made a certain decision. They illustrate why we should honor God and why it is unwise to ignore God's instruction. Angel legends also remind us that God is good and merciful and bestows favor, even honor, upon humanity. God's love toward human beings becomes evident in stories of the angels, because often the angels themselves must be convinced of humanity's place of honor in God's kingdom. In fact, angels most often came to no good when they resented humans or tried to dismiss them as mere mortals and therefore unimportant.

NATURE OF ANGELS

Angels are spiritual beings that serve God. That is central to Jewish belief about angels. Because angels are not trapped in mortal bodies, they are, in a sense, more spiritual than human beings are. Yet God bestows much favor and blessing upon humans, a fact that has at times met with angelic disapproval, or at least resentment. Ultimately though, angels serve God's purposes or they suffer the consequences. In Jewish lore and legend, not many angels carried their displeasure to the point of disobedience. They may have argued with God a few times, but they did relent.

According to Jewish texts, angels were created before people were; there is some disagreement as to timing. Some say they were created on the first day of creation; others say it would have had to be the second day—otherwise it might be implied that angels helped God with creation, and of course God did not need any help. Some say they were created on the sixth day. Still others suggest that angels may have been a sort of mold that God used to make humankind. In the Jewish community it is often said that angels are neither human nor divine; they are not like people, and they aren't like God. In other words, they are their own category, as God created them.

It is generally agreed that angels were made from light or from fire. Some legends place in heaven a river of fire—Rigyon—from which God makes the angels. They are immaterial, although they can, and do, sometimes take material form. They work within time and space but are not limited by either. Because they are not material, they have no need of food as we know it, but it has long been believed that they eat manna—the heavenly food that was sent down to the Israelites when they were hungry in the wilderness.

Jewish sources seem to agree that there are an infinite number of angels. No one knows how many there are. Some Jewish teaching claims that every person has not one but thousands of guardian angels. The kabbalists believe that every blade of grass has an angel.

As spiritual beings who reside in the heavens and are endowed by God with the ability to perform mighty works, angels are extremely powerful, having the ability to cause catastrophic changes in the earthly realm—such as instantaneous annihilation of cities such as Sodom and Gomorrah or the sudden destruction of an entire army.

One would think that, if angels have superhuman powers such as these, they would also be super-intelligent. This is true to an extent. They possess much wisdom and knowledge, much more than mortals do; however, they do not possess *all* wisdom and knowledge. Many secrets are known by God alone. In fact even the angels who uphold God's throne—whom we might assume to be closer to the secrets of God than any other beings—cannot see God, much less God's knowledge, because God is surrounded by great clouds of darkness and glory. It has been speculated in Jewish and other literature that all angels do not have identical knowledge; what they know is determined by which heavenly hierarchy they reside in, and which type of work they are given to do.

And although angels are, compared to humans, very wise and knowledgeable, they are not infallible. Some legends tell us that angels at times fight among themselves, and they have been known to make bad judgments.

Certainly, if the world had been left in the hands of the angels, most Jewish texts agree that humanity wouldn't have made it this far. Read, for example, this little story:

> When God wished to create man, he first created a company of ministering angels and said to them: Shall we make man in our image?"
>
> They asked, "Master of the Universe, what will be his character?"
>
> God replied, "Righteous descendants will come forth from him." But He did not report to them that wicked descendants would come forth as well. . . . God destroyed the first two groups of angels because they didn't consider mankind worthy to be created. The third group asked God what happened to the other two. In some versions of the legends, the angels formed parties and sects over the question of whether man should be created. While the angels argued, God created man.
>
> —creation myth, *Tree of Souls: The Mythology of Judaism*

To an extent, angels and heavenly life mirror life on earth. For instance, in heaven the Sabbath is kept. Angels sit at Sabbath tables and celebrate just as humans do. They are even monitored by a higher heavenly being who decides if the angels are celebrating appropriately; if they are, they are spared returning to, and being consumed by, the River of Fire.

According to one theory, guardian angels mirror the people they guard. In essence, we are given angels that are similar to us in personality. It would seem that this could prevent an angel's being objective enough about a person's behavior—but then again, a guardian is more likely to be lenient with a human with whom the angel shares certain characteristics or personality traits.

ANGELS AND HUMAN BEINGS

The angels may not have been enthusiastic about the creation of humanity, but according to one prominent Jewish legend, when God instructed the angels to bow down to Adam, the only one who refused to do so was Satan. For this disobedience God cast the angel out of heaven. Satan's revenge was to tempt and deceive Adam and Eve. Thus we have in the Jewish tradition the genesis of angelic opposition to the human race. Clearly, this opposition is also, in a sense, opposition to God, who created and blessed humanity. This theme will be developed further in chapter 6, "How Angels Fell."

For the most part, however, angels have always been considered helpers of humankind. While their first service is to God, in their obedience to God's will they, as a matter of course, look after the welfare of people. Because, once people were created, their care became a major responsibility for the heavenly hosts. Legends place various angels in the life of the first couple. For instance, angels acted as midwives to Eve, and the angel Michael gave important instructions to Adam and his sons.

In Jewish tradition, each person has a guardian angel. One of the more prominent beliefs is that each person has two guardians, one on his right and the other on his left. In a certain legend, on the eve of every Sabbath each man is accompanied by an evil angel and a good angel as he walks home, and the angels pronounce curse or blessing on his home, depending on how well the family is observing the Sabbath when they arrive.

Another common belief about guardian angels—held by those in the Hasid and kabbalist traditions—is that four angels accompany each person by the nature of their direction. Uriel guides from the east, Michael from the south, Raphael from the west, and Gabriel from the north. In this way, no matter where a person goes, he or she is wrapped in angelic protection.

Furthermore, entire nations have angels assigned to their welfare. It has been said that God will not punish a nation before he punishes its guardian angel—which implies that guardians are not only to protect their human charges but influence, as best they can, what humans do, moving or inspiring them to follow God's ways. Not surprisingly, angels are especially interested in the affairs of Israel. According to one legend, the angels cannot sing in heaven until the people of Israel sing first on earth. On the occasions when God sought to punish Israel, it was the angels' task to speak in Israel's defense; even if they didn't change God's mind they mourned the judgment.

In caring for humans, angels are said to keep marvelous records of human behavior. Angels record our deeds, whether good or evil. It's assumed that these record books will be brought forth as evidence on the Day of Judgment. But lest we think angels are merely out to get us, supplying a record of our misdeeds, we must also note that they carry our prayers to heaven. They present our prayers at the throne of God. Sometimes, they even intercede for us.

It stands to reason that if angels serve as our guardians and witnesses, then they are present from the beginning to the end of life. It's said that they are present when a baby is conceived, when that child is born, and on through life. And, although, historically, there has been disagreement within Judaism about the existence of an afterlife, any such belief includes the presence of angels. Angels watch over people while they die, and then the angels carry the souls of the deceased to their final resting place, whatever resting place that might be.

In some respects, Judaism ascribes to angels quite an influential role in the lives of mortals. For instance, in Jewish tradition there is a longstanding relationship between angels and the patriarchs. Various legends have angels tutoring Adam, Enoch, Noah, and Abraham, initiating them into wisdom about earthly matters as well as secrets of the heavenly realms. Angels accompanied the patriarchs to heaven, a time or two without a patriarch's experiencing death, as when Enoch suddenly disappeared from earth, Elijah rode into heaven on a chariot, and Moses was given a tour of heaven before he received the Torah.

Sometimes humans have, through mysticism, taken the initiative to interact with angels and angelic realms. One reason Judaism has produced so much literature involving angels is that its earliest form of mysticism—Merkabah—involved journeys whereby a person traveled through the seven heavens and to the throne of God. Ezekiel's vision of seeing God's glory in the Temple was a key text in this mystical tradition. The pseudepigraphical writings ascribed to Enoch recounted the patriarch's journey to heaven and helped establish the belief that, upon entering heaven, the patriarchs are transformed into angels. The third book of Enoch is sometimes called the Book of Palaces, relating to the seven levels of heaven that are constructed like concentric fortresses, with forbidding angels at each gate. An accomplished mystic could traverse these gates and ultimately find himself in the center-most palace, at the throne of God. Whether these were believed to be truly out-of-body experiences or altered states of consciousness, the topic was for centuries reserved for only the most learned. (It has been said that, even outside the context of any school of mysticism, the study of that visionary passage of Ezekiel was one of the passages saved for last when young boys were being instructed in Torah—because it involved an intense meditative state.) Thus, in the mysticism of the Jewish tradition, interaction with angels becomes more pronounced and detailed. Humans are able in some cases to transcend earth's boundaries, enter the heavens, travel with the angels, and perhaps even become like them.

A number of the early mystics, such as Eleazar of Worms, were said to have been in contact with angels and been informed by them. This tradition goes far back to the Book of Raziel, a text supposedly given to Adam by the angel Raziel, full of information about angels and heaven but also information about how to live on earth. It followed that knowing the names of angels was of significant benefit, and so within mysticism grew the practice of calling angels by name. Because they were God's angels and of course would do no evil, this conjuring, though frowned upon by the rabbis, was not considered evil, simply dangerous. It was thought that angels could act on their own and that a person could conjure an angel if he knew its name. Of course, any task given the angel by God would supersede human requests.

While their primary responsibility toward humans is to guard and protect us, sometimes angels become instruments of God's judgment upon us. Avenging angels and angels of destruction cause catastrophe, defeat armies, and bring plagues. Here's a particularly vivid account:

> One angel stands at one end of the world, and another stands at the opposite end, and they throw wicked souls back and forth, causing them to wander ceaselessly.
>
> —*Tree of Souls: The Mythology of Judaism*

Many of Judaism's beliefs about angels are similar to those of Christianity and Islam. It's important to note, however, that in order to study angels we must chiefly rely upon the traditions, legends, and scriptures rather than new or "groundbreaking" material. In recent centuries, doctrines about angels have not been prominent in Jewish life, for much the same reason they receded in other religions: The great golden age of angels was over. With the Age of Reason came skepticism about the heavenly host, and only a few mystics maintained any strong engagement with the topic.

However, the heightened interest in angels that has developed in the popular culture of the past half-century or so is reflected in present-day Judaism. Discussion of, and study about, angels has become more frequent in today's Jewish communities. Some of this interest no doubt grows out of the curiosity fed by the many popular movies, books, and television programs on the topic. Perhaps some Jews, in their quest to connect more deeply with their heritage, have discovered the wonderful treasury of angel lore as they read about their tradition. It's also possible that interest in angels is but one sign of the profound hunger many of us experience for some manifestation of spiritual realities. Fortunately for us, whether Jewish or otherwise, the presence of angels and their actions in our midst have remained constant, regardless of human perception or interest.

Three
ANGELS IN CHRISTIANITY

There have been ages of the world in which men have thought too

much of angels . . . [and have] honored them so perversely as to

forget the supreme worship due to Almighty God. This is the sin

of a dark age. But the sin of what is called an educated age, such

as our own, is just the reverse; to account slightly of them, or not

at all; to ascribe all we see around us, not to their agency,

but to certain assumed laws of nature.

—JOHN HENRY NEWMAN

*I*n the Christian Bible we find very little explanation of
angels. Mainly we have stories of angelic encounters.
Our theology has evolved almost solely from those.
Theologians back to the beginning of the church have
read between the lines as much as they dared, and except
for Thomas Aquinas they didn't generate much material
on the heavenly host.

EARLY CHURCH TEACHING

The topic of angels was not a high priority in the early
church. At its origins, the church was a Jewish sect,
comprised of followers of the Jew, Jesus of Nazareth, and
so of course they carried into this new faith their Judaic

perspective about the universe. The concept of an afterlife—with heaven and the angels—was not so firmly established as we often assume it was; in Judaism there was real tension between the Pharisees' belief in the afterlife and the Sadducees' denial of it. So even as the Christian faith spread and became its own entity, the big issues for leaders and theologians had to do with the divinity of Christ and the reality of resurrection. Angels had made appearances in the life of Christ, and in the early days of the church angels came to the aid of apostles who had been imprisoned; thus the reality of angels became established within the Christian story right away. It would be hard to determine any exact Christian doctrines about angels at that time, but we can assume that these Jewish followers of Christ brought to their new faith the traditional Jewish beliefs about angels: They were spirits created by God to carry out God's work in the world, and sometimes that work involved bringing messages to people, coming to their aid, or delivering God's judgment.

We find some scattered references to angels in documents of the early church. In the first century, Ignatius of Antioch said that he had only begun to "understand heavenly things, and the places of the angels, and their gatherings under their respective princes, things visible and invisible." At about the same time, Pope Clement I reminded Christians to "consider the whole multitude of his angels, how they stand ever ready to minister to his will." He also pointed out that, since God punished even the angels, humans would be subject to judgment: "The heaven is not clean in his sight: how much less they that dwell in houses of clay. . . ?"

A century later, we hear from Justin Martyr and Clement of Alexandria. Justin Martyr, in his First Apologia, taught that angels came forth from Christ, follow Christ, and are "made like to" Christ. He also mentioned those angels who followed the serpent (referring to Satan) and would thus be destroyed. Clement of Alexandria noted, among other things, that angels were sent to help our reasoning and to strengthen our hearts.

One of Clement's students was Origen, who, outstanding philosopher and thinker that he was, urged people toward a reasoning perspective about angels: "For to invoke angels without having obtained a knowledge of their nature greater than is possessed by men would be contrary to reason. But . . . let this knowledge of them, which is something wonderful and mysterious, be obtained. Then this knowledge . . . will not permit us to pray with confidence to any other than to the Supreme God, who is sufficient for all things." Origen seemed confident that, the more people understood about angels, the more they would be compelled to honor God and trust in God. He also recognized that angels were individuals and given specific duties: "as to Raphael, the work of curing and healing; to Gabriel, the conduct of war; to Michael, the duty of attending to the prayers and supplications of mortals. . . . [o]ne angel was to be Peter's, another Paul's."

Angels were further defined in the fourth century through the writings of such teachers as St. Basil the

Great, St. Cyril of Jerusalem, and St. Ambrose. St. Basil made the point that angels were not holy by nature but attained holiness, which they received from the Holy Spirit. The early Church Fathers perceived angels as created beings in the category of things "invisible" referred to in the Nicene Creed (325 CE); angels were not equal with God and were able to sin just as people were. St. Cyril theorized that angels were manifestations of God's glory but that, ultimately, they were beyond human understanding. And St. Ambrose considered angels mortal to the extent that they were created beings and not inherently *im*mortal—that is, God could choose to end their existence; this is the position St. John of Damascus took three centuries later. In harmony with other Church Fathers, John recognized the angels as spiritual beings possessing certain powers and qualities far beyond human limitations; yet the angels themselves were limited by God's own design.

Overall, church leaders of the early centuries were in agreement about the nature of angels and how they functioned among humans. Here and there would be a differing theory on some aspect of angelic existence, but the foundational beliefs—that they were creatures that either served God or opposed God and then acted toward humans accordingly—remained constant.

Even with such teaching to guide them, some Christians became too enthusiastic about these heavenly spirits, to the point of seeking connection with the angels as though they were deities in their own right. As early as the second century, St. Irenaeus was reminding Christians that it was God, and not the angels, who created the world. During the fourth century, Pope Damasus I proclaimed, "we are baptized only in the Father, and the Son, and the Holy Spirit and not in the names of archangels or angels." (Synod of Rome, c. 382).

The Christian church had to balance its teaching about angels so that, while heresy must be dealt with, proper recognition of angels must be maintained. The second Council of Nicea [787 CE] included angels in the list of entities that could be venerated and of which holy images could be made. Also on that list were Jesus, Mary, saints, and holy men. Such images "must be suitably placed in the holy churches of God, both on sacred vessels and vestments, and on the walls and on the altars, at home and on the streets." This was not simply a nice decorating option for religious people. It was important to church life that these images be displayed, and it is significant that angels were to be so remembered and represented.

The tone of early Christian writings that involved angels was generally respectful but cautious. Angels were spiritual beings created by God for specific purposes. They accompanied the Lord Jesus Christ, they gave help to Christians, and they surrounded God's throne in heaven, praising God constantly. Yet they were in no way equal to God and were not to be worshiped as people worshiped God.

Numerous writings of the early Church Fathers emphasized the presence of angels at baptism, the pivotal event in the life of a person turning from sin to God and the church. Early liturgies—worship services and rituals—assumed the presence of angels during worship, and angels were mentioned and addressed within the liturgies. Christians have always considered that humans join into a sort of partnership with angels when they are in the act of worship or any other ritual of faith.

The Christian Church was affected by the superstition of the Middle Ages, just as Judaism was. Scholars theorize that documents such as the Book of Raziel and the books of Enoch had Christians as authors or editors, and the early Church accepted some writings bearing angel information that were later excluded from the canon. Malcolm Godwin puts it well in *Angels: An Endangered Species*:

It was during . . . the 12th and 13th centuries, that the occult and esoteric embellishments reached truly exotic heights. By this time angels not only governed the seven planets, the four seasons, the months of the year, the days of the week, but also the hours of the day and the night. Spells and incantations abounded to conjure up both benign and bedeviled entities. By the 14th century there were said to be 301,655,722 of the host hovering at the borders of our temporal universe. 133,306,668 of these were of questionable help to the faithful as they were supposedly those who had fallen.

DIONYSIUS AND AQUINAS

When the apostle Paul preached in Athens, a man by the name of Dionysius was a member of the court who heard Paul and was converted. He worked with Paul in service to the Christian community, and Paul eventually appointed him to preside over the church in Athens. According to tradition, Dionysius preached extensively throughout what is now Western Europe, and he was martyred for the faith. The night before his execution, he and his companions celebrated the Divine Liturgy with angels.

Dionysius, known through the centuries as Dionysius the Areopagite, wrote many works about the faith and spirituality, four of which survived: *On the Celestial Hierarchy, On the Ecclesiastical Hierarchy, On the Names of God, On Mystical Theology.* The first of these taught about heaven and the angels, setting forth a hierarchy of nine angelic ranks.

In recent decades, scholars have determined that a first-century Christian could not have been the author of these works. Because of this, Dionysius the Areopagite was labeled Psuedo-Dionysius, and this is how he appears in various reference works. However, the Church Fathers had already absorbed these teachings. More significant, the great theologian Thomas Aquinas took them to heart.

We really cannot study angels in the Christian tradition without spending considerable time with Thomas Aquinas. He stands head and shoulders above any other teachers, philosophers, and writers when it comes to this topic. In his *Summa Theologica,* Aquinas dedicated scores of questions to the nature and ministry of heaven's hosts. He drew heavily from Scripture and the writings of Dionysius, Augustine, Jerome, and other Church Fathers. His material on angels goes on for hundreds of pages, earning him the title of "the Angelic Doctor." The work of Aquinas became foundational to the Christian faith, whether Catholic, Protestant, or some variation on one of those, and any "orthodox" belief about angels likely started with Aquinas or was at least reaffirmed by him.

Following is a simple summary of Aquinas's doctrine on angels. I have combined much of Aquinas's phrasing with my own paraphrasing in an effort to form a general commentary on these beliefs and what they continue to mean to us.

Nature of Angels

Angels were made by God; that is, they did not exist from eternity but were made. And they were created within the material realm because they would be related to it. "It was fitting for the angels to be created in the highest corporeal place, as presiding over all corporeal nature." It's obvious from the fall of some of the angels that they were not automatically holy when they were created. According to the book of Job, God found error in his angels (Job 4:18). Angels can be proud; Satan wished to be like God. The angels needed grace in order to turn to God. Aquinas quotes Augustine: "Who wrought the good will of the angels? Who, save Him Who created them with

His will, that is, with the pure love wherewith they cling to Him; at the same time building up their nature and bestowing grace on them?"

After an angel's first act of charity, it becomes a holy angel. After that, it cannot sin.

Angels are spirits. They are not material, do not have bodies. However they sometimes assume bodies; even then, their assumed bodies do not function as human bodies. For instance, they don't actually eat food (Tobit 12:19).

Angels do exist in places but it's not the same existence as a body with material dimensions has. Although they are spirit, their power and nature are finite—they are not infinite, as God is. So an angel cannot be in two places at one time, and two angels cannot occupy the same space. Again—they are not material in the same way humans are, yet they do occupy space in their own way.

Angels do move from place to place, although their movement is not the same as the movement of something material, such as a human body. An angel's movement does not correspond with heavenly bodies in the way that life on earth is affected by stars and planets. (Although some descriptions of angels found in Scripture include wings, angels would have no need of wings for actual flight because they don't move as material beings do. Church teaching maintains that wings on depictions of angels serve to symbolize their ability to move wherever they are sent rather than representing real wings with which to fly.)

An angel is made up of substance, power, and operation. An angel is created and therefore has substance, even though it is spirit. And apart from its substance it has power, which enables it to perform God's will. An angel does not merely exist but operates in the universe according to the tasks assigned to it by God. So an angel is a real being that acts in the world through the power it has received from God.

Angels do have intellect and will; intellect and will are not connected to organs of the body, and so an angel can have both these things (yet, we might wonder what Aquinas would say today, given modern-day studies about the physiological aspects of the mind and will).

There are thousands of angels, and they are of various species. In other words, not all angels are alike in what they know, what they are capable of doing, and what God has given them to do in the universe.

Angels, Knowledge, and Will

Angels have knowledge but do not collect or develop it as humans do. They are simply imparted with knowledge. There can be neither deception nor falsehood in an angel's knowledge. And angels of higher species (closer to God's presence) understand more than do the lower angels. Thus angels can impart information to one another, the higher to the lower. And all angels can know God, that is, they can have knowledge of God's existence and character; such knowledge is intrinsic to their nature. They do not acquire knowledge about God in the way people do.

Angels are given knowledge about God; in a sense, their knowledge is pure intelligence. In contrast, a human's knowledge of God involves experience, learning, and moral choices that put a person in the position to understand spiritual realities.

Angels can talk with one another and enlighten one another in that they can reveal truth to one another. Lower-rank angels can speak to higher-rank angels; in fact, any angel of any rank can speak to God.

Here's what angels do not know: future events and the secrets of hearts—these are known by God alone. Neither do the angels know the mysteries of grace. That is, angels do not experience the work of the Holy Spirit as humans do. People are moved by the Spirit to understand spiritual realities, to become sorry for evil behavior and to turn away from evil and toward God's goodness. People are spiritually reborn through God's grace (goodness and help) and are able to experience a profound inner transformation that makes it possible to know God in a very personal way. By their very nature, angels have no need of such an inner transformation. They are created to do God's bidding, and—as far as we know—do not wrestle inwardly to follow God. They communicate with God because they are created to do so, whereas people must go through a process of learning and enlightenment in order to perceive God's presence and be in communion with God. It's impossible to fully describe the "mysteries of grace"; but we know that angels do not partake of God's grace in the way people must. Even so, the angels want to know about these things (1 Peter 1:12).

Here's an excerpt that gives us some idea of just how intricately Aquinas explored angelic life:

> As in the ordinary day, morning is the beginning, and evening the close of day, so, their knowledge of the primordial being of things is called morning knowledge; and this is according as things exist in the Word. But their knowledge of the very being of the thing created, as it stands in its own nature, is termed evening knowledge; because the being of things flows from the Word, as from a kind of primordial principle; and this flow is terminated in the being which they have in themselves. [The expression "morning and evening knowledge" originated with Augustine.]
> —Summa Theologiae Pt.1, Question 58, Article 6

There is "no irascible or concupiscible appetite in the angels." Irascible and concupiscible appetites are connected to the senses rather than pure intellect. Yet the angels do possess natural love. They can love themselves, and their ultimate love is for God.

There are three hierarchies of angels, and within each hierarchy are three orders. Within one order are many angels. The distinction among the orders is not just a matter of gifts and functions but also a matter of nature; angels are not all of the same species. (See more about the hierarchies in chapter 5, Where Angels Dwell.)

Angels' Interaction with Human Beings

All material things are ruled by angels. But matter does not obey the mere will of an angel. God rules all, and the angels obey God. And matter obeys God ultimately, but God sometimes chooses to work through angels to deal with the material world.

God alone works miracles. Even when angels perform wonders, they are acting out of their created natures, not above and beyond their created natures. And sometimes angels act upon nature in a manner that that is simply beyond human knowledge; thus angelic action is not really a miracle because it is still within the bounds of created nature.

Angels can enlighten a person, but only God can change a person's will.

Angels can give revelation to people in dreams, and in this way angels interact with human imagination. Angels can also act upon the physical senses, both inside and outside a person. So an angel can change the weather, move objects, and so on, and an angel can also act upon what is inside the body—blood, temperature, and so forth.

God sends some angels to minister to people. Some of the higher ranks of angels, however, do not interact with human beings or, for that matter, with earthly life. In earth's realm, some angels assist while others administer. An angel that is in charge of a particular city is, in a sense, an administrator.

Each person is guarded by an angel. Jerome stated: "Great is the dignity of souls, for each one to have an angel deputed to guard it from its birth." Angels guard all people. Guardian angels come from the lowest rank of angels, which is called simply "angels." Angels guard people in order to "regulate them and move them to good." The guardian never forsakes the person. "The demons are ever assailing us, according to 1 Peter 5:8: 'Your adversary the devil, as a roaring lion, goeth about, seeking whom he may devour.' Much more there do the good angels ever guard us." And because angels are "perfectly happy," they do not grieve over the actions of the people they guard. We might think of them as devoted to our welfare while at the same time detached from us emotionally.

> For those benefits which are conferred by God on man as a Christian, begin with his baptism; such as receiving the Eucharist, and the like. But those which are conferred by God on man as a rational being, are bestowed on him at his birth, for then it is that he receives that nature. Among the latter benefits we must count the guardianship of angels.
> —Thomas Aquinas, *Summa Theologica*

There has yet to be produced a volume of material on angels that goes beyond what Aquinas and his colleagues produced. The present Christian theology of angels remains close to what those scholars formulated centuries ago.

SAINTS AND ANGELS

There's a long history of saints—Christians judged to be particularly holy and close to God—experiencing visitation by angels. It's impossible to separate biography from legend in many cases. But the prevalence of angels in lives of the saints has helped shape church doctrine about them.

Common are stories of Christians being assisted or comforted during imprisonment and martyrdom. In this category we find St. Agnes, virgin martyr, who was stripped of her clothing by her persecutors but then covered with a white robe by her guardian angel. St. Catherine of Alexandria was imprisoned and starved, but angels brought her food. Saints Cosmos and Damian were thrown into the sea and were rescued by angels.

According to several stories, angels have not only fed people but also have given them communion. One legend places Mary Magdalene in the desert for thirty years, doing penance for her sins. Not only was she fed daily by angels but was given last communion by them as she was dying. The wealthy St. Omobuono once gave away all his provisions on a journey, including his bread and wine. But angels put more bread in his bag and his flask miraculously filled with wine when he stopped to fill it at a spring. It's said that an angel brought Holy Communion every Sunday to St. Onuphrius the hermit. Agnes of Montepulciano was said to have had many visitations by angels, who occasionally brought her Holy Communion.

We have various stories of angels giving instructions to people. St. Anne, the mother of the Virgin Mary, could not conceive and of course prayed about this. An angel told her to go meet her husband, who was returning from a journey, because she would conceive. She did so, and became pregnant with the future Mother of Our Lord. One legend has the angel Gabriel appearing to Mary when she is an old woman, to prepare her for her death, which was but three days away. An angel once gave to St. Giles a scroll on which was written the secret sin that King Charlemagne could not bring himself to confess. An angel told St. Stephen where to preach and indicated to St. Humility which convent she was to join.

Angels are famous for carrying people or things to other places. When St. Catherine suffered a martyr's death by decapitation, angels carried her body to a monastery. When St. Barbara converted to Christianity, angels carried her away to hide her from her angry pagan father. St. Veronica was carried to heaven by the angels. And, believe it or not, the foreskin of the circumcised baby Jesus was said to have been carried by an angel to Charlemagne, who enshrined it in a church.

A number of times, angels are said to have given witness or verification to believers. Marrying in obedience to her parents' wishes, St. Cecilia asked her new husband to respect the vow she had taken to remain a virgin. She told him that an angel guarded her. He asked to see this angel, and he not only saw the angel bring to them lilies and roses, but he also heard the music of angels. When St.

Dorothea was on her way to execution, one man mocked her, asking if she might bring him fruit from the garden in paradise. When the saint died, an angel appeared to the man and gave him fruit and flowers, both out of season. When the irritated master of the peasant Isidore was about to complain about the lost work time due to the saint's prayers, he saw two angels plowing in Isidore's place.

Numerous saints had visions of angels: Agnes of Montepulciano, Angela of Foligno, Claire of Montefalco, Francis of Assisi, Gregory the Great, John de Matha, and Teresa of Avila, among others. One of the most impressive stories is of Frances of Rome, whose guardian angel was visible to her for twenty-three years. She's reported to have said, just before her death: "The angel has finished his work. He is beckoning me to follow."

And some saints were allowed to hear the angels sing. St. Ignatius of Antioch began the practice of antiphonal singing because he heard the angels sing that way. The story has it that people could hear angels singing as they carried to heaven the soul of St. Martin of Tours, and they sang at the funeral of St. Thomas of Canterbury.

And at least once the angels took the celebration a bit further: It's said that they danced with St. Vitus.

Recent Teaching of the Catholic Church

In 1925, Pius XI wrote the Encyclical *Quas primas,* in which he pointed out "not only that Christ is to be adored as God by angels and men, but also that angels and men obey and are subject to His power. . . ." The encyclical was about the kingship of Christ, and in explaining this he placed the angels in their proper place as worshipers of God rather than objects of human worship. Twenty-five years later, Pius XII touched briefly upon the topic of angels in an encyclical sent to clarify several issues. The document was something of a catch-all for various errors occurring in church teaching at the time. Evidently some people were questioning that angels were "personal creatures," which they are according to church doctrine.

The next time there is any significant mention of angels in Catholic documents is in 1986, when Pope John Paul II composed six articles, known as Catechesis on the Holy Angels, in response to wide-ranging beliefs about angels that were being generated in popular culture. He says as much, in the opening of article one:

Today, as in times past, these spiritual beings are discussed with greater or lesser wisdom. One must recognize that at times there is great confusion, with the consequent risk of passing off as the Church's faith on the angels what does not pertain to it, or, vice versa, of neglecting some important aspect of the revealed truth.

John Paul II's 1986 articles cover the basic doctrine on angels: They were created by God, at the same time the material world was created. They are entirely spirit, although they sometimes take material form. And because they are spirit only, they are closer to God—more like God—than humans are. They also have intellect:

> The pure spirits have a knowledge of God incomparably more perfect than that of man, because by the power of their intellect, not conditioned nor limited by the mediation of sense knowledge, they see to the depths the greatness of infinite Being, of the first Truth, of the supreme Good. [Article 2, #3]

And, according to the Catholic Church, angels have free will, by which some of them turned away from God, rebelling against heaven and becoming fallen angels, or demons.

Scripture refers to angels personally, as in the cases of Michael, Gabriel, and Raphael, who are named in specific narratives. Angels are also referred to by groupings, such as Cherubim, Seraphim, and Principalities, which determine the primary tasks the angels are given.

Angels serve two major purposes. One is to praise God, to be always in God's presence. The other is to help human beings, according to God's purposes. One way angels have helped humans is by participating in the several events in the life of Christ that led to salvation. An angel told Mary that she would give birth to Christ; angels sang and communicated with people at Christ's birth. They ministered to him after his great temptation in the wilderness and in the Garden of Gethsemane on the night before his death, and they were present at his resurrection and ascension. Thus angels have taken part in the salvific history of the world, acting as messengers to people and as helpers to Christ.

Angels will come with Christ when he appears at the Second Coming; they will assist him in judging the world. And angels will play roles on both sides of the final battle between good and evil, with God's angels accompanying Christ to destroy the fallen angels, the chief of them being Satan.

[W]e understand how the Church could come to the conviction that God has entrusted to the angels a ministry in favor of people. Therefore the Church confesses her faith in the guardian angels, venerating them in the liturgy with an appropriate feast and recommending recourse to their protection by frequent prayer, as in the invocation "Angel of God." [Article #4]

THE ORTHODOX CHURCH

Mortals cannot begin to understand the freedom of the holy angels and the scope of their intellects, untrammeled by physical brains. Crystal clear and faultless, knowing no pain or frustration, unhindered by doubt or fear, neither male nor female, they are beauty, love, life, and action welded into individual unutterable perfection.

—Mother Alexandra, *The Holy Angels*

There is no substantial variation between Orthodox and Roman teaching on the angels, but Orthodox Christianity is probably more conscious of their role. In the Orthodox Church, angels are venerated on the level of saints, and when an Orthodox person is baptized and chooses a patron saint, that saint is afterward called the person's angel. One of the most thorough, recent books exploring Orthodox doctrine on angels is *The Experience of God: Orthodox Dogmatic Theology, Vol. 2* by Orthodox scholar Dumitru Staniloae.

The 35th Canon of the Council of Laodicea condemned and forbade the worship of angels, yet made the distinction between worship and veneration. It has thus been Orthodox practice to pray to angels as intercessors and helpers.

Guardian angels have some prominence in Orthodox belief and practice. It is believed that every child receives a guardian at birth, and that the guardian accompanies that person at death—after entering heaven, the person will recognize the guardian. It is not unusual for an Orthodox Christian to pray specifically to his or her guardian angel.

In concert with Roman Catholics, the Orthodox believe that nations have guardians as well, and that when a church is consecrated, it receives a guardian angel.

The Archangel Michael is a major hero for Orthodox Christians. They dedicate to him churches and monasteries, and he is invoked for protection against enemies. He is assumed to be the angel present, though not always named, in various biblical narratives, including the Exodus accounts of the pillars of fire and cloud and the story of the Hebrew youths in the fiery furnace.

Daniel B. Clendenin offers a beautiful statement describing angels in *Eastern Orthodox Theology*:

> Guardian angels are especially our spiritual kin. Scripture testifies that the guardianship and direction of the elements, of places, of peoples, of societies, are confided to the guardian angels of the cosmos, whose very substance adds something of harmony to the elements they watch over. According to the testimony of Revelation, the angels share, constantly and actively, in the life of the world, as well as in the life of each one of us; by becoming attuned to the spiritual life we can hear these voices of the world beyond and feel that we are in touch with them. The world of angels, which we know at our birth and which is therefore accessible to our remembrance . . . opens to us on the threshold of death, where—according to the belief of the church—the angels greet and guide the soul of the departed.

PROTESTANT BELIEFS

Mainline Protestant Christianity has adopted, at least unofficially, beliefs about angels that predate the

Reformation. The topic of angels was not part of the great dispute between the Church of Rome and the Christians who split from it in the sixteenth century. And just two centuries after the Reformation came the Enlightenment and Age of Reason, when angel lore was relegated to the place of superstition and simple legends, at least in the minds of many educated people, including the many seminary students who would become pastors and leaders in mainline Protestant churches. We don't find any great Protestant treatises on angels in recent centuries.

However, the Bible remained of utmost importance to this new branch of the church called Protestantism. Protestants believed that Scripture should be available to, and read by, all believers, not just the clergy. And because of the many specific references made to angels in the Bible, belief in them endured. Because of the Protestant emphasis on Scripture as the sole authority on faith, however, belief in angels was limited to only what could be found in Scripture pertaining to them. This created a different understanding of the topic than what developed in Catholic and Orthodox congregations.

Protestant evangelical churches, in general, have maintained polite acknowledgment and acceptance of angels. Because of their strong adherence to Scripture to the exclusion of any other writings or teachings, these Christians are among the least likely to wander off into angel worship or to seek an occult understanding of, or conversations with, angels. However, Scriptures provide numerous stories of human encounters with angels, and so Christians who come from more fundamentalist traditions do not question that such encounters still happen. The Scripture stories open a way for them to experience the existence of angels without violating their avowed boundaries of belief and practice.

In the Pentecostal and Charismatic branches of the church, many are comfortable with the idea of angels because firsthand experience of the "supernatural" is normal and widespread. Speaking in tongues, the laying on of hands for healing, receiving visions and prophecies—these experiences accustom believers to perceiving power and wisdom from beyond normal human means. In such circles people talk freely of encounters with angels just as they might speak of receiving a word from the Lord during prayer or in a dream. These Christians, however, are also bound to strict scriptural tradition when it comes to angels. So while they may freely welcome angel encounters, they will consider it an occult practice when someone claims to help people talk directly with angels or to seek guidance from them.

It's important to note that these same Christians who take the Bible literally and as the sole source of information when it comes to angels also believe in demons, or fallen angels. From time to time within the Protestant church there is a surge of interest in the battle between the hosts of heaven and hell.

For the general Christian population, certain teachers and preachers have done much to shape our everyday thinking about angels. In the United States in 1975, Billy

Graham published *Angels: God's Secret Agents,* which became a bestseller. A Baptist and not, by his own profession, a theologian, Graham relied chiefly on passages from the Bible, and he related the stories of some people who had encountered angels. Twenty years later, Professor Peter Kreeft of Boston College published *Angels (and Demons): What Do We Really Know about Them?* based upon, primarily, the teachings and traditions of the Roman Catholic Church. What these books have in common is their popular style and their adherence to established Christian doctrine. Many similar books have appeared during the past century.

Four
ANGELS IN ISLAM

[T]hy Lord inspired the angels, (saying:) I am with you.

So make those who believe stand firm.

—The Qur'an, 8:12

"To speak of Islamic spirituality from its most popular to its most esoteric level is to call attention to the role of the angelic hierarchy." So states one scholarly text on Islam. Angels are so important to this religion that that they are included in a key passage of the Qur'an:

[R]ighteous is he who believeth in Allah and the Last Day and the angels and the Scriptures and the Prophets. (2:177)

Likewise, the unrighteous person is described thus:

Say (O Muhammad, to mankind): Who is an enemy to Gabriel! For he it is who hath revealed (this Scripture) to thy heart by Allah's leave, confirming that which was (revealed) before it, and a guidance and glad tidings to believers;

Who is an enemy to Allah, and His angels and His messengers, and Gabriel and Michael! Then, lo! Allah (Himself) is an enemy to the disbelievers. (2:97-98)

Angels enjoy enough prestige in Islam that, when the name of a major angel is invoked, it is generally followed by "upon him be peace," the same phrase which follows the mention of a prophet. The Islamic declaration of faith, or the Shahadah, does not name angels specifically, but according to Ira G. Zepp:

> [There are] five main elements of faith, which are subsumed under the Shahadah: 1) belief in one God, who alone is worthy of worship; 2) belief in angels, spiritual beings who do the will of God; 3) belief in sacred books, including the Torah, the Psalms, and the Gospel; 4) belief in the prophets . . . 5) belief in the Day of Judgment and resurrection."
> —*A Muslim Primer: Beginner's Guide to Islam*

The Muslim prayer that is performed five times daily contains one element, the salaam, which acknowledges the guardian angels present: "Peace be with you, and the mercy of Allah."

The Qur'an, Islam's sacred text, names these angels: Gabriel and Michael, both Archangels, Harut and Marut, Malik, and Ridwan. Other angels named in Islamic tradition are Israfil, Izra'il, Munkar and Nakir, along with numerous others, found deeper in the mystical/magical branches of the faith.

Not surprisingly, Islamic belief about angels is similar in many ways to those of Judaism and Christianity; the three faiths share the same patriarchs, prophets, and stories.

Angels were created by God, to carry out God's will in the universe, to help and encourage human beings, and to assist God in works both in heaven and on earth.

In Islamic belief, angels were made from light, whereas humans were made from clay. While angels are superior to humans in intellect, humans are considered ultimately superior because they are made in God's image and, unlike the angels, have been entrusted with free will.

After God created Adam, he instructed the angels to prostrate themselves before this marvelous creation. All but one bowed down to Adam; Iblis refused, saying to God, "I am better than him. Thou createdst me of fire, whilst him Thou didst create of clay" (Surah 38:77). For this sin of pride, God cast Iblis out of heaven, and thereafter he became the tempter of Adam and Eve.

There's some discrepancy among sources about Iblis, also known as the devil or Satan (Shaytan). Some claim that because he was made from fire, he was not an angel but chief of the jinn, a lower spirit form. The jinn are a class of spirits made from smokeless fire. Because they have free will, they can be good or evil, and they have been known to help people but also act hostilely toward them, even possessing them at times, similar to demons of Christian cosmology. However, jinn are not beyond saving; in Surah 72, a band of jinn is converted when the jinn listen to God's revelations.

So Iblis/Satan was either one of the jinn all along or was demoted to that status after refusing to bow before Adam. The Qur'an calls Iblis an unbeliever, one who opposes

God and tries always to lead people away from God. At the end of Surah 38, Iblis says to God: "I surely will beguile them every one, / Save Thy single-minded slaves among them" (vs. 83-84).

To which God replies: "I shall fill hell with thee and with such of them as follow thee, together" (vs. 86).

Islamic belief places guardian angels around every person, and it assumes the presence of angels as our constant witnesses, who listen to our prayers, record our deeds, and carry our souls to their destinies, whether in Paradise or Hell. They will be involved in the Day of Reckoning, presenting to God books in which are written all human deeds. According to tradition, angels accompany the soul as it leaves the body, question it as to the person's faith, and, if the person is a believer, takes the soul to heaven for a preview, and then returns it to the grave until the end of time, final judgment, and resurrection.

> "Lo! those who say: Our Lord is Allah, and afterward are upright, the angels descend upon them, saying: Fear not nor grieve, but hear good tidings of the paradise which ye are promised.
>
> We are your protecting friends in the life of the world and in the Hereafter. There ye will have (all) that your souls desire, and there ye will have (all) for which ye pray." (Surah 41:30-31)

We don't find quite as much systematization of the angelic world in Islam as in the hierarchies of Catholicism or the elaborate mystical constructs of Judaism. In "The Angels," a chapter of *Islamic Spirituality: Foundations,* Sachiko Murata cites a work by al-Qazwini (*Marvels of Creation,* Cairo, 1374) that summarizes various types of angels based upon "the Qur'an, the Hadith, and later tradition":

1) Bearers of the Throne, four angels appearing as eagle, bull, lion, and man, that hold up God's throne.

2) The Spirit, which occupies one rank, while the remaining angels together occupy another rank. Some traditions place this angel over all the others.

3) Israfil, who delivers commands, places spirits within bodies, and will blow the trumpet on the Last Day.

4) Gabriel, who delivered the Qur'an to Muhammad.

5) Michael, charged with providing nourishment for bodies and knowledge for souls.

6) Izra'il, the angel of death.

7) Cherubim, who turn away from everything but God, and glorify him night and day.

8) Angels of the seven heavens.

9) Guardian angels, of which each human being has two.

10) Attendant angels, who descend upon humanity with blessings and ascend with news of their works.

11) Nakir and Munkar, who question the dead in their graves.

12) The journeyers, who visit assemblies where men remember the Name of God.

13) Harut and Marut, who were given human sensibilities

and sent to earth, to test whether or not angels would sin if they were sensual as humans were.

14) Angels charged with each existent thing. Only God knows how many there are.

(p. 327, adapted)

The Qur'an contains more than one hundred references to angels. It presents stories quite similar to the Genesis account of creation and the fall and the account of the annunciation found in the Gospel of Luke. Angels are represented as surrounding God's throne, acting as messengers to humans and also bringing judgment against them.

Judgment is a major theme in Islam. On the Day of Judgment will be the great reckoning. Thus, what people do in this life is of utmost importance. Mohammad preached repentance in ways similar to what Jesus preached.

In *Life after Death: A History of the Afterlife in the Religions of the West*, author Alan Segal makes an interesting point:

The dead are not able to contact the living hence no one is to be consulted in the grave . . . (Sura 35:19–22; 27:80). This is meant to arrest universally popular spiritualism. On the other hand, the living can visit the afterlife [with its attending angels], both in dreams and visions, because that warns humans about what awaits believers and nonbelievers after death.

Outside of the Qur'an's sacred text is the Hadith, writings of the prophet Muhammad or by others about him. Certain references to unnamed, non-specific angels in the Qur'an are developed further in the Hadith. For instance, the Qur'an tells us that angels will question and even torment the dead; in the stories and teachings of the Hadith appear Munkar and Nakir, two angels who come to a person's grave four days after death and interrogate him.

Much of Islam's material about angels has come out of its mystical branch, Sufism. For centuries, Sufi writers have generated various theories about the nature of angels and their positions in the universe. One of the great Sufis, Ibn 'Arabi, made many references to angels in his writings, particularly *The Meccan Revelations*. For instance, out of 'Arabi's teachings came the theory that the four Archangels are connected to the four basic attributes of God: Life (Israfel), Knowledge (Gabriel), Will (Michael), and Power (Izra'il).

Sufis, like the Jewish and Christian mystics before them, were known to have visions of angels and heaven; some considered this part and parcel of the mystic's journey along the path of enlightenment. Not surprisingly, the work and experience of Sufis was sometimes criticized and questioned by Islamic scholars and clerics. The great fourteenth-century Islamic scholar Ibn Khaldun wrote an assessment of Sufi practice in his *Muqaddimah: An Introduction to History*. Part of his work is quoted in *Judaism, Christianity, and Islam: The Works of the Spirit:*

The Sufis discuss four topics. (1) Firstly, they discuss pious exertions, the resulting mystical and ecstatic experiences, and self-scrutiny concerning one's actions. . . . (2) Secondly, they discuss the removal of the veil and the perceivable supernatural realities, such as the divine attributes, the throne, the seat, the angels, revelation, prophecy, the spirit, and the realities of everything in existence. (p. 257)

Ibn Khaldun handles this second matter, that of "removing the veil," by saying that in essence these experiences are subjective and intuitive and cannot be understood by people to whom they do not happen, so it's best not to criticize them. He seems to have reached a conclusion fairly similar to that of the Church Fathers, who, while they weren't always rejoicing when someone reported hearing voices or seeing apparitions of the Holy Mother, decided that unless the person veered off into sin or heresy, the experience did not merit or command any official judgment.

In Muslim cosmology, an angel is required for everything that happens, including the digestion of food. They are believed to correspond to ten levels of intellect, and they have been credited with not only the movements of planets but also the formation of a raindrop. According to some Islamic teachings, one group of angels deals only with God and has no contact with earthly matters, including humans, while a second group deals with humanity and its immediate environment.

Muslims believe generally that, while angels have more knowledge than humans and are closer to God due to their purely spiritual makeup, humans are still superior because they are made in the image of God. And while angels deserve our recognition and respect, they are not to be worshiped (Surah 3). We are to worship God alone. The angels are servants of God and exist to serve God's will.

Islamic tradition tells us that angels bring us courage; they are present whenever we gather to remember God or to pray. When our deeds are good, they praise God; when our deeds are evil, they ask God to forgive us. The Qur'an states that God can send thousands of angels to our aid. One poetic summary is offered in Surah 42, verse 5:

Almost might the heavens above be rent asunder while the angels hymn the praise of their Lord and ask forgiveness for those on the earth.

Five
WHERE ANGELS DWELL

Journeys to heaven

appear in both Jewish and Christian folklore.

Souls are borne by birds, by angels, by a chariot of light, by boat,

or by rope, ladder, arrow, chain, tree, or plant, or on horseback.

Souls ascend pillars of smoke and light, climb a mountain,

or pass through a window. . . .

The saved dwell with angels or even become angels themselves.

—JEFFREY BURTON RUSSELL,

A History of Heaven: The Singing Silence

When the religions of Judaism, Christianity, and Islam were formed, the earth was still considered the center of the universe. Everything beyond human reach was "up" or "down." And the worlds in either direction were imagined to have palaces, courts, and hallways similar to what people had experienced on earth. There were levels of paradise or descending regions in the land of the dead; between those levels were borders that could not be crossed except by those who were worthy. And even the most esteemed of the worthy had to be accompanied by spirits who inhabited those realms.

SPHERES OF HEAVEN

In the Greco-Roman world, among intellectuals and philosophers, the belief prevailed that the higher in the heavens one moved, the purer the substance one would find there. Upward were ether and light, and the spiritual rather than the material. As one moved down toward earth, substances were weightier, more material, and less pure. The more pure a person's soul, the higher up he or she might progress. This concept of matter, spirit, and purity was incorporated, if informally, into the world-views of many people of the time, regardless of religion or creed.

Although there were variations on the layout of the spheres, most believers and philosophers settled on the number seven. Since the earliest days seven has been considered a symbol of holiness and completion. And seven was the number of heavenly bodies that were visible before technology made it possible to peer far into space.

In Jewish lore and tradition there are seven levels of heaven, seven levels of earth, and seven of hell. The seven levels of heaven are as follows:

The Curtain (Vilon): This is the partition between earthly and heavenly life.

The Firmament (Raki'a): The sun, moon, and stars are placed in this heaven.

The Clouds (Shehakim): Legend tells us that in this place great millstones grind manna for the righteous.

The Lofty Abode (Zebul): This is upper Jerusalem, a mirror of the earthly Jerusalem; here the Archangel Michael makes offering on the altar in the Temple.

The Dwelling (Ma'on): The ministering angels (as opposed to those that remain around God's throne) dwell in this heaven.

The Fixed Place (Makhon): All manner of precipitation is stored here, along with storms and fire.

The Thick Darkness (Aravot): This is the highest heaven, where God dwells with many angels, with the souls of the righteous, and with souls not yet born. Darkness in this instance is not associated with evil or the absence of light, but rather with mystery and unfathomable holiness.

There is also a legend of an eighth heaven, above all others, in which are mysteries known to God alone. And there is a great heavenly curtain, the Pargod, which separates God, in his Holy of Holies, from all else, including the angels.

Generally, heaven was believed to consist of concentric layers or atmospheres, and the highest (farthest from earth) was also the holiest, because it was closest to God. This image was based in part on human conventions, such as the court of a king. There is the inner sanctum, where the king sits upon his throne, and only certain people are allowed in his presence. Outside that throne room is a hallway or courtyard, and a few more people can enter there. And farther out from the throne are other rooms and courtyards, until, out beyond the palace altogether, common folks are free to come and go.

Thus was heaven imagined, with its highest, most holy level right around the throne of God. The first two or three levels beyond that are still outside the realm of anything mortal; only in the lowest heavens do the creatures of heaven—the angels—have much to do with people at all.

In Islam, the doctrine of the Five Divine Presences lays out a similar map of the universe. One version is elaborated upon in *The New Encyclopedia of Islam* and roughly adapted here:

Hahut: the Godhead, or Absolute Reality
Lahut: Personal God
Jabarut: the realm of the angels
Malakut: the realm that merges spiritual and physical (magic and psychic experiences happen here)
Nasut: the human world

It's important to note that, in all three faith traditions, mystics have been known to traverse the heavens, whether through dreams, visions, or out-of-body experiences. And accounts of these journeys have often revealed seven heavens. The prophet Enoch traveled through seven; the prophet Mohammad did as well, and Paul speaks of his journey (he didn't know if it was an actual journey or a vision). This consistency points to common literature and legend; it also points undoubtedly to something deeper, perhaps even archetypal. Some people argue that these are "only myths"—meaning that they are not true—because they show up everywhere and are not the property of only one faith tradition. Another possibility to consider is that the prevalence of certain themes throughout culture points to a truth that transcends individual creeds and is shared by many traditions.

HIERARCHIES OF ANGELS

Given that heaven has its levels, the angels also have their hierarchies. The angels around God's throne are a different species from the ones that take human form and visit us mortals at times. In each of our three faiths of Abraham there has been this distinction. And although the numerous hierarchies that have developed do not match, their intent is the same: to distinguish among the various angels according to their functions in the universe and their closeness to God.

It stands to reason that in Judaism with its seven heavens there have been seven ranks of angels. The listings vary, according to source. Here are two:

1) Chayyot (Holy Creatures)
2) Seraphim (Fiery Ones)
3) Sarim (Princes)
4) Cherubim (Mighty Ones)
5) Ofanim (wheels)
6) Irinim (Watchers, High Angels)
7) Malachim (messengers/angels)

---

1) Cherubim
2) Seraphim

3) Ofanim
4) all the angels of power
5) Principalities
6) the Elect One (Messiah)
7) elementary powers of the earth and the water

However, the seven ranks of angels do not necessarily correspond to the seven heavens; the angels usually exist in one or two of the heavens, for example those angels around God's throne and the angels in the lower realms who deal with the material world.

An additional angelic hierarchy of ten ranks has been identified within the Jewish mystical tradition of the Kabbalah. The tree of Ten Holy Sefiroth (loosely, the attributes/manifestations of God) is sometimes shown with an Archangel identified with each of its branches.

In Islam, the angels have not been ranked as specifically, but there are the different functions of angels, such as throne bearers, as in Judaism and Christianity, and also Archangels. Regardless of any ranking system, the functions of angels in all three faiths are very similar.

Within the early Christian Church, angelic hierarchies proposed by various notables—such as St. Jerome, St. Gregory the Great, and St. Ambrose—have not been consistent with one another. It's worth noting that the early Church Fathers worked from a number of documents that were eventually excluded from the canon, some being the same sources that fed Jewish lore and tradition.

The early Church Fathers did speculate on a fairly sophisticated cosmology, whereby the angels were created before humanity and the material universe in a realm that was itself eternal and apart from what we know as time and space. As Dumitru Staniloae explains in *The Experience of God: Orthodox Dogmatic Theology*: "St. Basil spoke of a kind of state older than the creation of the world, supra-temporal, aeonic, eternal, one proper to the supraterrestrial powers. It is in this state or aeon that the author and creator of all things will have created the spiritual, invisible creatures." Still, the angels would not be eternal in the way God is, not co-existing before all things as God did, but in an existence apart from the material universe.

The hierarchy most widely accepted in Christianity was put forth by a writer identified as Dionysius the Areopagite, a convert of the apostle Paul. Most scholars today place the writing a few centuries later; thus the writer is often referred to as Pseudo-Dionysius. One of his chief works, *The Celestial Hierarchies,* maps out the heavens and ranks the angels. Regardless of the writer's real identity or the actual date of the composition, his version of angel realms was adopted by most of the Church Fathers; most important, it was adopted by Thomas Aquinas, who wrote the seminal treatise on angels within his *Summa Theologica.* And, because the scholarly study of angels disappeared with the coming of the Enlightenment, Aquinas's work has remained the standing definition.

The church fathers and mothers accepted the hierarchy of Dionysius because it was well reasoned and supported by Scripture. However, some were wise to point out that this hierarchy was likely not comprehensive. As Chrysostom put it, "There are in truth other powers, whose names even are unknown to us." Overall, the topic of angels has been regarded as mystery, and most teachers have been careful not to be terribly dogmatic about its details.

Here then, are the nine "choirs of heaven" as put forth by Dionysius and developed further by Aquinas:

1) Seraphim
2) Cherubim
3) Thrones
4) Dominions (also known as Dominations)
5) Virtues
6) Powers (also known as Authorities)
7) Principalities
8) Archangels
9) Angels

The nine choirs comprise three triads. Tradition gives each a major function. The first triad, made up of Seraphim, Cherubim, and Thrones, worships God continually. The second triad, comprised of Dominions, Virtues, and Powers, rules the universe and its elements. These first two triads have little, if anything, to do directly with human life. The ranks of the second triad take instruction from those in the first. And those in the second triad communicate with the ranks of the third triad.

The third triad, made up of Principalities, Archangels, and Angels, deals with humanity and matters here on earth.

Tradition has attributed certain characteristics to each rank of angels; some of these are supported by Scripture.

Seraphim are described in Isaiah 6:1–3:

I saw the Lord sitting on a throne, high and lofty; and the hem of his robe filled the temple. Seraphs were in attendance above him; each had six wings: with two they covered their faces, and with two they covered their feet, and with two they flew. And one called to another and said:

"Holy, holy, holy is the Lord of hosts;
the whole earth is full of his glory.

The Seraphim are considered to represent pure love for God. They are often depicted as having many eyes. They are also considered to facilitate, or at least to represent, purification. In this same vision of Isaiah, the prophet realizes that he is a "man of unclean lips." One of the Seraphim flies down with a live coal and touches it to Isaiah's mouth and says, "Now that this has touched your lips, your guilt has departed and your sin is blotted out."

Cherubim, too, are winged. Some scholars speculate that representations of Cherubim were fashioned after the statues of monsters that guarded palaces in Babylon, where the Jews were exiled. We have a detailed description of Cherubim in the Ezekiel 1:4–14:

> As I looked, a stormy wind came out of the north: a great cloud with brightness around it and fire flashing forth continually, and in the middle of the fire, something like gleaming amber. In the middle of it was something like four living creatures. This was their appearance: they were of human form. Each had four faces, and each of them had four wings. Their legs were straight, and the soles of their feet were like the sole of a calf's foot; and they sparkled like burnished bronze. Under their wings on their four sides they had human hands. And the four had their faces and their wings thus: their wings touched one another; each of them moved straight ahead, without turning as they moved. As for the appearance of their faces: the four had the face of a human being, the face of a lion on the right side, the face of an ox on the left side, and the face of an eagle; such were their faces. Their wings were spread out above; each creature had two wings, each of which touched the wing of another, while two covered their bodies. Each moved straight ahead; wherever the spirit would go, they went, without turning as they went. In the middle of the living creatures there was something that looked like burning coals of fire, like torches moving to and fro among the living creatures; the fire was bright, and lightning issued from the fire. The living creatures darted to and fro, like a flash of lightning.

Some traditions of Christianity have attributed the many-eyed Cherubim with enlightenment and wisdom.

Thrones are named such because they bear the throne of God. They may be the Ofanim named in the angelic lists of Judaism. Thrones are named specifically, along with Dominions, Principalities, and Powers, in Colossians 1:15-16, in what was probably a hymn of the early church:

> [Christ] is the image of the invisible God, the firstborn of all creation; for in him all things in heaven and on earth were created, things visible and invisible, whether thrones or dominions or rulers or power—all things have been created through him and for him.

Thrones have been characterized as ministers of God's justice.

Dominions, according to Dionysius, organize and govern the duties of all angels under them. Tradition gives them the function of helping earthly rulers govern wisely.

Virtues (possibly Tarshishim of Judaic literature) are said to be courageous. They are sometimes depicted with four wings and wearing armor. They help mortals to be courageous as well, and from the Virtues come blessings and miracles. It was a belief of the early Church that Virtues assisted those humans, such as leaders of nations, who were put in charge of others, the theory being that administrators needed additional help and wisdom.

Powers, which are also known as authorities, battle demons and work for the protection of humanity. Although Powers have been represented with swords, there is no description of them—or of Dominions or Virtues—in Scripture.

"Rule and authority and power and dominion" are mentioned in Paul's letter to the Ephesians (1:21). Principalities and Powers are named in Colossians 2:15:

[Christ] disarmed the rulers and authorities and made a public example of them, triumphing over them in it.

When the Scriptures speak of Christ in *opposition* to these angel ranks, they refer to the fallen angels, which, though now opposed to God, still exist as distinct species and possess the functions with which they were first created.

The third triad of angels—consisting of **Principalities, Archangels, and Angels**—is much more involved with humanity than are the first two. Tradition tells us that Principalities are set over the nations; there is some support for this in Daniel 10:13, where an angel tells Daniel that he started to come to Daniel's aid from the first day Daniel prayed but "the prince of the kingdom of Persia" prevented him. "The prince of the kingdom of Persia" has been interpreted to mean the angel who was in charge of Persia. Only when another angel, Michael, intervened, could the angel sent to help Daniel complete his mission. Judaism and Christianity have generally supported belief in angel guardians of nations. (Trends in Pentecostal and Charismatic belief have adopted the idea of territorial demons as well as angels.)

The **Archangels** are often considered princes in heaven's hierarchies. In Judaism and Christianity, the princes over specific ranks of angels have been named but there are variances in these lists, and no direct reference to angels serving as leaders of ranks is made in the canon of Scripture. The closest we come to identifying an angel as a leader of other angels is in the New Testament book of Revelation, where Michael is called the commander of heaven's armies.

The term Archangel occurs only once in the Bible, in the New Testament book of Jude, verse 9, which gives this title to Michael. According to the Apocryphal book of Tobit and the New Testament book of Revelation, seven angels stand before God. In Christianity, these are considered the seven Archangels. The three named in Scripture are Michael, Gabriel, and Raphael; tradition has given us Uriel, Chamuel, Zadkiel, and Jophiel.

However, these names vary according to tradition. One article on Orthodox belief by Fr. Michael Pomazansky (orthodoxinfo.com) suggests several names in addition to Michael, Gabriel, Raphael, and Uriel. In apocryphal writings we find Jeremiel, Salathiel, Phaltiel, Psaltiel, and "pious tradition" has named Jehudiel and Barachiel.

Jewish writings name four Archangels: Gabriel, Michael, Raphael, and Uriel. The pseudepigraphical writings of Enoch name seven princes (possibly

Archangels) of the seven heavens; however, the lists within the Enoch texts are inconsistent.

Islam claims four Archangels: Gabriel, Michael, Israfel, and Azra'il.

However many Archangels there are, and whatever their names, their functions remain constant. They are messengers from God who bring to human beings wonderful (and sometimes not wonderful) tidings. They reveal, in little glimpses and sometimes in elaborate visions, the mysteries of God and prophecies of what is to come. They help people understand God's will.

Angels are the lowest rank of the heavenly hosts, but they are the ones with whom we humans are most familiar. Even though they are the lowest in heaven, to us they are brilliant, overwhelming, and awe-inspiring. Whereas the news of Christ's coming birth was delivered by Gabriel, an Archangel, the more mundane information of daily life comprises the language of "ordinary" angels. When we receive a sudden intuition or hunch, when a sensation compels us away from danger, when an encouraging voice murmurs close by and helps us stay the course—we are receiving the help of angels. While the Seraphim hover in praise around the throne of God, angels walk alongside us through hard work and unforeseen danger. While the Dominions oversee the stars and winds, the angels provide a tow-truck from out of nowhere, or a kind, mysterious stranger to bring us aid or deliver words that we are desperate to hear.

It is true that heaven's map as we know it is a composite of beliefs and legends from times gone by, based upon dictatorial governments and primitive astronomy. This need not diminish our vision of heaven, however. Visions are given for a reason. And sacred Scriptures have proven trustworthy in the matters of this present life. It is possible that a few centuries from now we will stumble upon evidence that we consider more empirical than the dreams and stories we now believe. But in the absence of such data, and in light of our ongoing experience of God and the angels, we can rest our hearts and minds upon a heaven that is vast and layered, and filled with so many kinds of angels that we will never find names for them all.

Six
HOW ANGELS FELL

"I watched Satan fall from heaven like a flash of lightning.

See, I have given you authority to tread on snakes and scorpions,

and over all the power of the enemy;

and nothing will hurt you."

—JESUS, quoted in Luke 10:18-19

*N*o matter which holy text, legend, or theory you believe, all versions of the angels' fall have one thing in common: the angels' relationship to human beings. The Christian story is possibly the most kind, in terms of the beginning of the strife. The first we hear of the devil, or Satan, he is in the form of a serpent in the Garden of Eden, convincing Eve that all is not as God says it is. We get hints of the devil's beginning—Satan had once been an angel—in one or two passages of the later prophets, and only in the New Testament, in the Book of Jude, do we get a little more of the story:

The angels who did not keep their own position, but left their proper dwelling, he has kept in eternal chains in deepest darkness for the judgment of the great day. (v. 6)

But the real dirt on the devil is found in the legends of Judaism, in which we discover that the angels as a whole disapproved of the enterprise called humanity. They resented that God would give any sort of honor to these creatures made from simple earth. They were indignant about how physically weak we are, our bodies harboring all sorts of lusts and passions that lead to no good. Later, even the angels who had not fallen and who were in heaven with God were not at all happy when they learned that God was about to give Moses the Torah.

The event that led to the fall of some of the angels was God's requirement that they prostrate themselves before Adam. Some of the early scholars (including Thomas Aquinas) theorized that the angels made themselves holy by their first good act. They had the will and intellect to do good or evil, and once they chose either, that's what they became. If we hold to this theory, then perhaps the angels' first opportunity for good or evil was how they reacted to God's creation of the human race.

In Jewish lore, Satan refused to bow before Adam, declaring that the man was inferior to him. So God cast Satan—and the angels who, along with Satan, refused to bow—out of heaven. Satan came to the Garden of Eden to tempt Adam and Eve and thus have his vengeance.

This legend is repeated, with some adjustments, and becomes holy text in the Qur'an, appearing in at least two different places. In one, God tells the angels that Adam will be his deputy on earth, and the angels protest that God would make as deputy one who would "do evil and shed blood, when we have for so long sung Your praises and sanctified Your name." But God taught Adam the names of things, and this knowledge had not been given to the angels; thus Adam's superiority was proved. Whereupon God told the angels to bow before Adam, and all but Satan did so. In the next account, Satan (Iblis, in Arabic) argues that man is made from clay, and he, the angel, is made from fire, so he will not bow before the man. So God casts out Satan and his companions.

So at the heart of the angels' fall was pride, or envy; they did not want human beings to enjoy God's favor or the angels' honor. Lust also became a theme in the angels' downfall. According to a prominent Jewish legend, a lower rank of angels, called the Watchers, were placed on earth to help humans. They were teachers and guardians. But in the course of their work, they began to lust after human women. And some of the Watchers had sexual relations with the women. Out of these unions came the giants, or Nefilim, mentioned in Genesis 6:4.

The problem with this theory is that angels were considered to be spirit and genderless, and so how could they lust after human women? Some churchmen decided that the Watchers were actually a tenth rank of angels, who had material—and sexual—bodies. The Christians gave them the name Grigori.

In the book of Ezekiel, chapter 28 we have a portrait of Satan's pride and fall, folded within a prophecy about the evil king of Tyre:

Because you have been so haughty and have said, "I
am a god; I sit enthroned like a god in the heart of the
sea," . . .

You were the seal of perfection,
Full of wisdom and flawless in beauty.
You were Eden, the garden of God;
every precious stone was your adornment:
. . .
I created you as a cherub
With outstretched shielding wings;
And you resided on God's holy mountain;
You walked among stones of fire.
You were blameless in your ways,
From the day you were created
Until wrongdoing was found in you.
. . .
You grew haughty because of your beauty,
You debased your wisdom for the sake of your splendor,
I have cast you to the ground,
I have made you an object for kings to stare at.
(verses 2, 12-13, 14-15, 17, Tanakh)

Satan has been considered the prince of the demons, the
great angel who led many other angels astray. Many versions
of Satan exist in mythology and belief. Malcolm Godwin
presents a helpful summary of them in *Angels: An
Endangered Species*. Satan has been identified with the
Hebrew name of Apollyon, the angel of the bottomless

pit. He is also known as Sammael, the Angel of Death; as Belial, the ruling prince of Sheol; as Beelzebub (this name was applied earlier to a Canaanite deity); as Azazel, the chief of the Grigori; as Mastema, the Accusing Angel; and Lucifer, Prince of the Power of the Air, once the greatest angel.

It has long been believed that Satan was a great angel, perhaps the greatest, the first angel created, God's favorite. Because the order of Seraphim are considered to be those closest to God's glory, many have conjectured that Satan was the Archangel prince of the Seraphim before his fall from heaven. In Ezekiel 28:14, Satan is referred to as God's cherub, leading some to believe that he was the chief of the Cherubim.

According to tradition, Satan convinced a third of the heavenly host to rebel with him, and those multitudes became fallen angels, or demons.

DEMONS IN JUDAISM

In the Jewish tradition there is a legend about how, as God was finishing up creation on the eve of the Sabbath, he ran out of time before he could create bodies for all the souls he had made. These entities became demons.

The story of Satan's tempting Adam and Eve is well established in the Jewish faith, and the concept of fallen angels is certainly present, but the connection between bad angels and Satan is not as firm as it is in Christianity. Angels are angels, and very righteous and learned men have had the ability to deal with them.

In the chapter "Angels in Judaism" I described how the importance of knowing angels' names developed into the mystical practice of conjuring angels. At times demons were conjured as well, and the Jewish mystics/magicians created what was probably the most well-developed demonology of any Western religion. At the same time, they recognized that the demons remained under God's authority, and if demons were called upon it was to put them into service, not to seek their power or acknowledge any authority apart from the abilities natural to them.

Even so, folktales and superstitions worked upon the Jewish concept of demons. They were associated with any sort of uncleanness. There developed a tradition that no man traveled home alone after Sabbath prayers, lest he be attacked by demons. Demons were said to be especially present at key spiritual moments, such as birth, circumcision, marriage, and death.

During the Middle Ages, when demonology of all sorts flourished, Jews considered that they were constantly surrounded by demons, but they were for the most part generic spirits that had little to do with theology. Here and there a demon had prominence and a name, such as Lilith, the she-demon who tried to kill infants.

Because of the legend about demons' being spirits without bodies, it was believed that they sought bodies to live in. The more common belief, however, seems to have been in dybbuk, the spirit of a dead person who sought to inhabit the living. For spirit or demon possession there were exorcism rituals to be administered by the rabbis.

While there were various actions a person could take to avoid demonic harassment—such as not wandering around alone after dark—the preventative given by religious leaders was simply not to provoke the spirits by trying to conjure or use them.

DEMONS IN ISLAM

There's a wonderfully insightful definition of demonic work in *The New Encyclopedia of Islam:*

Among the traditional signs of "dark spirits" are the following: first, that they say the opposite of the truth; second, that they deny their own faults and attribute them to others, preferably to someone who is completely innocent; third, that they continually change their position in an argument, the purpose of argument being only to subvert, to turn aside from truth and goodness; fourth, that they exaggerate the evil of what is good, and the good of what is evil, that is, they define good as evil because of a shadow of imperfection, and evil as good because of a reflection of perfection; they glorify a secondary quality in order to make it an essential one, or to disguise a fundamental flaw; in short, they completely falsify true proportions and invert normal relations.

I don't believe I've ever read a better description of evil. It is significant that this comes under the entry of "Iblis," the Arabic name for Satan; there is no entry for "demons" at all. Islamic beliefs about demons are similar to those of Judaism and Christianity, in that demons are considered spiritual creatures that act with animosity toward humans. In Islam there is the added presence of the jinn, a lower spirit form that predated Islam (and Judaism for that matter). Because Islam was at its beginning primarily a religion of Arab tribes, it was laid over the animistic religions that predominated in the desert. Jinn were spirits that inhabited places and animals. They were not necessarily all bad or evil, but at the very least they were unpredictable and not to be trusted. This concept has been married somewhat to the Jewish and Christian idea of demons.

Islam recognizes demons to the extent that there are standard prayers against them. And the same Sufis who worked with magic and alchemy had their interactions with demons as well. But there does not seem to have developed the elaborate demonology as found in Judaism or Christianity.

DEMONS IN CHRISTIANITY

In Christianity, belief in demons has been maintained in proportion to belief in angels. If a person believes in the spiritual beings described in the Bible, then he or she must believe in both groups of those beings: the angels that continue to serve God and assist humans, and the angels that fell from heaven and continually harass humanity.

The traditional doctrine of Christianity places demons far below the Godhead, in that they are merely angels who rebelled. Christian orthodoxy does not propose an evil force equal to God's good force. Furthermore, the death and resurrection of Christ broke forever the power of Satan and the demons he commands. These forces of evil still operate in the world, but they are operating on borrowed time. At the end of time as we know it, the Last Judgment will finally settle the matter, and the fallen angels will be thrown into hell forever.

Just as the early Church Fathers and Mothers believed that much human knowledge had been imparted from God through the ministry of angels, and that angels had assisted humankind in progressing toward holy living, the church also believed that nations had been led astray by the fallen angels, or demons. The angels were created to help humanity progress toward a life of enlightenment and communion with God. Likewise those angels that fell attempted to accomplish the opposite of that, teaching humans false doctrines and introducing practices that would put entire societies off track. Jean Danielou explains further, in *The Angels and their Mission According to the Fathers of the Church*:

God entrusted the nations to good angels who taught them the religion of the true God as He makes Himself known in the movement of the heavens, but the evil angels turned them away from the natural religion and caught them in a net of perversion and idolatry. This explanation corresponds closely to the religious history of the pagan peoples as described in the epistle to the Romans. Eusebius here sketches a whole theology of the history of religions by distinguishing, among the non-Biblical religions, first a cosmic revelation, which is that of the true God; and then idolatry, which is the perversion of it.

In medieval times, scholars believed that there were archdemons as well as Archangels; this makes some sense, if we assume that fallen angels maintained their faculties originating from their angelic ranks. These seven archdemons were associated with the seven deadly sins:

Lucifer = pride
Mammon = avarice
Asmodeus = lechery
Satan = anger
Beelzebub = gluttony
Leviathan = envy
Belphegor = sloth

THOMAS AQUINAS ON DEMONS

As with looking to Thomas Aquinas for scholarship on the topic of good angels, we can turn to Thomas Aquinas for a summary of the Church's beliefs about demons. I have gleaned basic teachings from Aquinas's many pages on demons, incorporating them into a general commentary on how these teachings influence current Christian belief.

Aquinas asserts that, at one time, even the demons were good. But the devil sinned right after he was created. The sin of that highest angel caused other angels to sin as well. According to 2 Kings 6:16, the sinful angels were still outnumbered: "There are more with us [angels] than there are with them [fallen angels]."

Because demons were created as angels, they still have the natural gifts (faculties) they had as angels. And because the angels existed in various orders, they retained the gifts of those orders after the fall; thus there are different orders of demons, which more or less correspond to the orders of the angelic hierarchy. This supported the belief in archdemons mentioned in the previous section. We might assume that, as in the case of angels, there are demons that serve as princes or leaders of other demons. In the absence of clear teaching or evidence, it's impossible at this point to know if demons operate at the various levels of existence, with some working their evil against the cosmos on a larger scale and others concerning themselves only with human activity.

Aquinas acknowledged that demons do have some knowledge of the truth; this is reasonable to expect, because knowledge is, to a limited extent, the property of angels. In matters that lie beyond mortal understanding, demons undoubtedly have some advantage. Nevertheless, we must not confuse knowledge with enlightenment. True enlightenment issues from God's truth and from a relationship with God. Because the demons rebelled against God, they are unable to be enlightened or to enlighten others, whether fellow demons or human beings. This is one reason that Christian teaching has so forcefully discouraged people from seeking knowledge from demons, such as special charms or secret spells. While a demon may have real information about the universe, without the wisdom of God to accompany such information it is impossible to apply it to one's life in any helpful way.

Aquinas did not attribute to the demons any passions that are connected to the senses. In other words, demons do not experience fear, joy, or other emotions. However, they experience a certain kind of sorrow—that which is connected to the will. "Sorrow can be the will's resistance to what is or what isn't," states Aquinas. It was, after all, the will of these former angels that brought them into rebellion against God.

Christian orthodoxy asserts that the devil always urges people to sin. And the demons remain malicious toward God and human beings. On these points Aquinas is clear. The demons, having chosen evil, cannot reform them-selves or change their intentions but continue on their course of evil work.

Aquinas offers an interesting explanation of the rela-tionship between demons, sin, and God. A demon will assault a human out of sheer malice. But God orders the assault, because God knows how to make orderly use of evil and turn it to do good. So while God uses demons for God's own purposes, the demons are motivated by their own malice.

Until the judgment day, the ministry of the angels and wrestling with demons endure until then. Hence until then the good angels are sent to us here; and the demons are in this dark atmosphere for our trial; although some of them are even now in hell, to torment those whom they have led astray; just as some of the good angels are with the holy souls in heaven. But after the judgment day all the wicked, both men and angels, will be in hell, and the good in heaven.

Christians have taken demons seriously, thanks to Thomas Aquinas and other leaders of the faith. But they remind us that, ultimately, good angels have power over bad angels. God permits bad angels to commit some evil for good purposes, and the good angels "do not entirely restrain the bad from inflicting harm."

Current Belief about Demons

Christianity has consistently maintained that fallen angels are evil, in that they oppose God and seek the sorrow and destruction of humankind. Because they are angels, they are more powerful and more knowledgeable than people. But even though they are knowledgeable, they are also known to be liars, distorters of the truth, one of their primary goals being to deceive people and nations in order to turn them from faith in God and from living in righteousness and justice.

Many Christians consider this present world to be the focus of a massive war between the forces of good and evil. Believers in God's holiness and purposes are prime targets of those spiritual forces that decided long ago to oppose God. Not only are demons present, but also they are aggressive in their attempts to discourage faith, pre-empt good works, cause great suffering, and lead people to do evil against themselves and others.

The persistence of belief in demons is supported by the Gospels themselves, in which Jesus speaks often of demons and deals with them repeatedly as he heals the sick and delivers those who are possessed by evil spirits. The New Testament contains scores of references to demons. And angels scholar Maria Pia Giudici puts it bluntly in her book *Angels: Spiritual and Exegetical Notes*: "The Savior's way of acting would be totally inexplicable were Jesus not really convinced of the reality of Satan."

Skepticism about demons, and particularly about demon possession, has arisen with the advent of modern psychology. Yet theologians (and a few experts in other fields, such as psychologist M. Scott Peck) make a distinction between mental illness and demon possession. Here is how one Protestant writer describes possession:

> . . . projections of a new personality, supernatural knowledge . . . supernatural physical strength, moral depravity; in addition there may be deep melancholy or seeming idiocy, ecstatic or extremely malevolent or

ferocious behavior, spells of unconsciousness, and foaming at the mouth.
—Merrill F. Unger, *Demons in the World Today*

Terminology has developed in both Catholic and Protestant circles concerning levels of demonic activity with humans. *Temptation* arises in everyday life, and although a lot of temptation needs no demon behind it, some of it is believed to be manipulated by demons. *Oppression* takes the form of deep sorrow, doubt, or despair as well as overwhelming destructive circumstances and calamities. Sometimes when people are plagued by atypical illness or depression or strings of mishaps while in the midst of important ministry or spiritual progress, they suspect demonic activity. When we read the lives of the saints this certainly seems to be the case with some of them. *Possession* is considered rare and is defined as a demon's inhabiting the body of a human. Most Christian teachers and pastors consider that possession happens to people who have opened a door to demonic activity through persistent sin against God and resistance to repentance.

And some people believe that a true follower of God cannot be overcome by demons. This belief goes back at least as far as Origen (second century) who stated: "The true Christian who has submitted to God alone and to His Word, will suffer nothing from demons, for He [God] is mightier than demons."

The Catholic Church has specific procedures for exorcism, and we may think of demon possession as rare, but many dioceses have an exorcist. This person usually keeps a low profile or remains anonymous altogether to avoid drawing unwarranted attention to the work of exorcism or the topic in general. In Protestant congregations demon possession and exorcism are most often acknowledged and talked about in the more fundamentalist branches such as Pentecostalism, where exorcism is a less ritualized and regulated practice. In both situations, those who are experienced in this field will say that prayer and fasting are required and that exorcism should never be attempted alone but within a group of people who exhibit spiritual maturity and who work as a team.

It is tempting to dwell upon the angels who fell, because pop culture has portrayed demon possession and other evil activity as sensational and even glamorous at times. But Jews, Christians, and Muslims agree that preoccupation with the dark side is not our calling. It's important that we live with the awareness that evil exists; we must respect the power of the demons and their ability to scheme against us. But their influence is weakened and rendered impotent in the face of prayer and holy living. And—this is important to remember—we do not face them alone, because God's faithful angels fight alongside us. That the angels fight the demons on our behalf is but one of the many ways in which they assist us on our earthly sojourn.

Seven
HOW ANGELS MINISTER

Wherever innocence is most oppressed and trampled upon

is precisely where the angels are likely to intervene.

But also wherever correction or punishment is called for,

the angels are likewise apt to be present. . . .

They represent the two characteristic faces of the heavens at one

and the same time; they are either suffused with sunlight

or dark with menacing clouds;

in either case the help they send down upon the earth

is always beneficial.

—MARIA PIA GIUDICI, *The Angels: Spiritual and Exegetical Notes*

*W*e can't possibly know everything angels do. But scripture, tradition, and legend give us much evidence about some of their key tasks in matters regarding humanity and life on earth. It would make sense that angels carry on activities in the universe beyond our sphere, but we have only hints of what those activities might be. It is enough for us to know that they carry out the wonders of God wherever they are.

For now, we can take encouragement from the many ways in which angels encourage and help us in daily life, on this planet we call home.

ANGELS PRAISE GOD

One of the best-known accounts of a human's seeing angels is given in Isaiah 6. The prophet has a vision in which he is in the Lord's temple and God's glory fills the temple. And six-winged Seraphim hover there, crying out, "Holy, holy, holy is the LORD of hosts; the whole earth is full of his glory."

According to all three faiths, some angels exist to do nothing but praise God. These are higher orders of angels that do not deal with earthly matters or with human beings; rather, they exist all around God's throne expressing praise continuously. Isaiah's vision helped shape Jewish thought about this. A similar vision is recounted by St. John in the Book of Revelation, where he is caught up in the spirit and shown God's throne, around which creatures having six wings do not stop proclaiming, day and night, "Holy, holy, holy, the Lord God the Almighty, who was and is and is to come" (4:8).

In the Qur'an, it is said that the prophet "seest the angels thronging round the Throne, hymning the praises of their Lord," (Surah 39:75).

Of course, all angels praise God. But for some this appears to be their only duty.

There are myriad angels, however, whose primary purpose is to serve humanity and deal with earthly matters. The New Testament book of Hebrews says this succinctly: "Are not all angels spirits in the divine service, sent to serve for the sake of those who are to inherit salvation?" (1:14). This divine service falls into several categories.

Angels get sent to relay messages to human beings. Sometimes the human beings don't realize right away that they're talking to an angel. When the three angels came to Abraham and Sarah at Mamre (Genesis 18), announcing that Sarah would give birth to a son, they first appeared to be three strangers traveling through. In the lesser-known tale of an angel's visiting the wife of Manoah (Judges 13) the angel seems but a man, especially to Manoah, but he appears and disappears twice, the second time ascending into heaven on the flames of Manoah's burnt offering, at which point Manoah finally comprehends that this is a supernatural encounter (his wife had figured this out already). The angel's announcement on that occasion was to tell Manoah's wife that she, who was barren, would have a son.

There's no ambiguity whatsoever when a similar announcement is made to the priest named Zechariah in Luke 1 and to the virgin named Mary in Luke 2; in both cases the angel's arrival is frightening—and in both these cases the angel is announcing a miraculous birth to come.

We see annunciation scenes in the Qur'an that are similar to those in the book of Luke. However, in the Qur'an's account, Zechariah is struck dumb for only three days as a sign that Elizabeth will bear a son (in Luke he remains mute for the duration of the pregnancy, and this is a punishment for his lack of faith). And the Qur'an speaks of Mary's being visited by "Our spirit in the semblance of a full-grown man," of whom she is frightened until he reveals that he is God's emissary. He tells her that she will give birth to a son, and she asks how this could be so, because she is a virgin. The angel replies that this is an easy thing for God and that the son will be a sign to mankind and a blessing from "Ourself." Whereupon Mary does conceive, journeys to a far-off place and goes into labor under a palm tree. Evidently, she is not spared the agony of childbirth and prays to die, but a voice tells her that God has just put a brook at her feet, and if she shakes the palm trunk, fresh dates will drop into her lap. She must eat, drink, and rejoice.

Angels announce things other than births, but "the annunciation" has taken on its own meaning in the Christian tradition, since Gabriel appeared to the girl Mary. This summons, and Mary's response to it, has become a key text about joyful, human submission to the call of God in one's life.

Angels announce destruction, or they describe what is happening or about to happen—this occurs all through the Book of Revelation, in which angels explain the meaning of events in John's vision as they unfold.

ANGELS GUARD AND RESCUE US

He will order His angels
to guard you wherever you go.
They will carry you in their hands
lest you hurt your foot on a stone.
—Psalm 91:11-12, Tanakh

One of the most popular beliefs about angels is that they protect us from harm. The vast majority of present-day accounts of angelic encounters have to do with people's being snatched from death: invisible hands pulling a person out of the path of an oncoming car, a child being led by a light or voice or a kind stranger out of harm's way. In one account, a mountain climber lost in a blizzard is spared twice from falling over precipices by railroad crossing signs that appear out of nowhere and then disappear.

The Christian belief in guardian angels is based in part on a statement Jesus made in Matthew 18:10: "Take care that you do not despise one of these little ones; for, I tell you, in heaven their angels continually see the face of my Father in heaven." In the book of Genesis, the patriarch Jacob, when he is near death, offers a blessing upon Joseph: "The God before whom my ancestors Abraham and Isaac walked, / the God who has been my shepherd all my life to this day, / the angel who has redeemed me from all harm, bless the boys . . ." (Genesis 48:15-16).

St. Basil wrote, "We pray to God who is well disposed toward men in order that He might give an angel of peace as a companion to protect us." and also "An angel is put in charge of every believer, provided we do not drive him out by sin. He guards the soul like an army."

Belief in guardian angels is long established in Jewish, Christian, and Muslim doctrines about angels. In Jewish lore and tradition, each person is guarded by not one but thousands of angels. It is also believed that each person has one angel on his left and another on his right. Early Church Fathers proclaimed that every person was assigned a guardian angel at birth that accompanied the person throughout life. The Qur'an states that each person has an angel in front of him and one behind.

The nations were believed to have their guardian angels as well. These angels are called ethnarchs or archons. St. Basil, St. John Chrysostom, and Pseudo-Dionysius are among the early Christian thinkers who were convinced that, based on Scriptures such as Deuteronomy 32:8 and Daniel 10:13–21, each nation had its guardian angel who not only watched over a people in the physical sense but was held responsible for the spiritual direction they took. This belief certainly predated the Christian church, originating with the ancient Jewish teaching if not earlier.

Beyond guardian angels are those sent to rescue people, especially righteous people, who are in danger. When the three Hebrew youths are thrown into the fiery furnace in Daniel 3, a fourth "man" appears, looking different from the others—witnesses recognize him as looking like "a divine being" (Tanakh). A few chapters later, when Daniel is thrown into the lions' den, an angel comes to shut the lions' mouths, and Daniel survives the night.

In one story, a misguided prophet is rescued from his own plans. Balaam is on his way to meet with Balak, who wants the prophet to curse the people of Israel and thus protect the interests of Balak's tribe. Balaam knows God's will in this matter, that he is not to curse the Israelites, and he has told Balak this, but Balak sent "more numerous and more distinguished" messengers, and Balaam asked God a second time if he should go. God said to go but to do only what God told him to do. But from what follows, it seems that God was quite angry that Balaam came back a second time when he already knew the answer:

> God was incensed at his going; so an angel of the LORD placed himself in his way as an adversary.
>
> He was riding on his she-ass, with his two servants alongside, when the ass caught sight of the angel of the LORD standing in the way, with his drawn sword in his hand. The ass swerved from the road and went into the fields; and Balaam beat the ass to turn her back onto the road. The angel of the LORD then stationed himself in a lane between the vineyards, with a fence on either side. The ass, seeing the angel of the LORD, pressed herself against the wall and squeezed Balaam's foot against the wall, so he beat her again. Once more the angel of the LORD moved forward and stationed himself on a spot so narrow that there was no room

to swerve right or left. When the ass now saw the angel of the LORD she lay down under Balaam; and Balaam was furious and beat the ass with his stick.

Then the LORD opened the ass's mouth, and she said to Balaam, "What have I don't to you that you have beaten me these three times? Balaam said to the ass, "You have made a mockery of me! If I had a sword with me, I'd kill you." The ass said to Balaam, "Look, I am the ass that you have been riding all along until this day! Have I been in the habit of doing thus to you?" And he answered, "No."

Then the LORD uncovered Balaam's eyes, and he saw the angel of the LORD standing in the way, his drawn sword in his hand; thereupon he bowed right down to the ground. The angel of the LORD said to him, "Why have you beaten your ass these three times? It is I who came out as an adversary, for the errand is obnoxious to me. And when the ass saw me, she shied away because of me those three times. If she had not shied away from me, you are the one I should have killed, while sparing her." (Num. 22:22–33, Tanakh)

This rich little tale brings a couple of concepts to the fore. One is that angels often are charged with protecting us from ourselves. The other is that animals are probably much more aware of spiritual presences than are humans. There's plenty of anecdotal material indicating that animals and small children are often able to perceive angels when adults remain oblivious to them. Of course, this is a story, a legend, in which a donkey talks and his owner is so caught up in his own anger that he seems not to notice that he's conversing with his own beast of burden. And the angel is highly frustrated with Balaam and would have killed him but let the donkey live because the poor thing was doing its best to serve its master and avoid annihilation.

The persistence of the angel in the Balaam story is reminiscent of another story in Genesis concerning Lot, the nephew of Abraham. The three angels come to Sodom to judge its fate, and when it is clear that the city must be destroyed, the angels tell Lot to take his wife, daughters and their husbands and flee the city immediately. Lot relays the message to his sons-in-law, who don't take him seriously, and the next morning, the whole family is still in Sodom. "So the men [angels] seized him and his wife and his two daughters by the hand, the LORD being merciful to him, and they brought him out and left him outside the city" (Genesis 19:16).

Angels showed up in the life of Jesus Christ several times according to Gospel accounts (see "Jesus" in the Encyclopedia), and he was aware of their continuing presence. From his words in Matthew 26:52-53, we see that he acknowledged their guardianship on a grand scale. He had just been arrested, and one of his disciples tried to defend Jesus by drawing a sword:

> Then Jesus said to him, "Put your sword back into its place; for all who take the sword will perish by the

sword. Do you think that I cannot appeal to my
Father, and he will at once send me more than twelve
legions of angels? But how then would the scriptures
be fulfilled, which say it must happen in this way?"

Shortly after the death and resurrection of Jesus, his
followers experienced the help of guardians, particularly
when being associated with Jesus became dangerous.

Then the high priest took action; he and all who were
with him (that is, the sect of the Sadducees), being
filled with jealousy, arrested the apostles and put them
in the public prison. But during the night an angel of
the Lord opened the prison doors, brought them out,
and said, "Go, stand in the temple and tell the people
the whole message about this life." When they heard
this, they entered the temple at daybreak and went on
with their teaching. (Acts 5:17–21)

Judging from the contemporary stories of angel
encounters, it would seem that the majority of cases
involve protection or rescue of some kind. In the collective
mind at least, guardian angels are very much present to us
today as in past centuries.

Angels Intercede for Us

There's a marvelous story in the Muslim tradition
about the angels protesting when God showed favor to

humankind. Why would God love creatures that were so sinful? God explained to them that humans were sinful because of their sensuality; it was very difficult to exist in the material world without going astray. God went so far as to say that if the angels were given human traits, they, too, would sin.

The angels rejected this idea. No—they would never sin as humans did, even if they were given human sensibilities. So God allowed them the opportunity to prove this. The angels chose Harut and Marut, two of the most humble, worshipful angels in heaven, and they sent them to earth, endowed with physical bodies and therefore subject to the material world.

Eventually, Harut and Marut committed all the sins of which humans were guilty. Ever since then, the angels have interceded for human beings, asking God's forgiveness for our sins.

In Jewish tradition, angels intercede for us, and they especially intercede for the people of Israel. In fact, some legends claim that angels opposed God at times when God was about to judge Israel or bring calamity upon the nation for its sins.

In the book of Zechariah, the prophet reports that "the angel of the LORD exclaimed, 'O LORD of Hosts! How long will You withhold pardon from Jerusalem and the towns of Judah, which You placed under a curse seventy years ago?' The LORD replied with kind, comforting words to the angel who talked with me" (Zechariah 1:12-13, Tanakh). Here we glimpse the passion with which heaven's hosts observe human history. Jesus focused this idea even more when he said in Luke 15:7, "I tell you, there will be more joy in heaven over one sinner who repents than over ninety-nine righteous persons who need no repentance."

We find a classic reference to angelic intercession in the book of Tobit. The angel Raphael has disguised himself as a distant relative in order to assist Tobias on a journey. At the end of the tale, Raphael reveals his identity and says, "When you and Sarah prayed, it was I who brought and read the record of your prayer before the glory of the LORD" (Tobit 12:12).

ANGELS ACCOMPANY AND GUIDE US

In the Book of Tobit, just mentioned, the Archangel Raphael goes on a journey with the young man Tobias. Raphael is a good companion who teaches Tobias and helps him understand what he must do. This theme appears in many stories and legends. Jews, Christians, and Muslims have incorporated into their thinking that we are never really alone but are always accompanied by the angels, who seek to help us do what we must do and overcome obstacles along the way.

The company of angels was established early in Jewish history, in the story of the great Exodus from Egypt. The newly freed Hebrews, known also as Israelites, were accompanied through the wilderness by an angel that appeared as a pillar of cloud by day and a pillar of fire by night.

I am sending an angel before you to guard you on the way and to bring you to the place that I have made ready. Pay heed to him and obey him. Do not defy him, for he will not pardon your offenses, since My Name is in him; but if you obey him and do all that I say, I will be an enemy to your enemies and a foe to your foes. (Exodus 23:20–22, Tanakh)

When we consider how difficult it would have been for an oppressed people to set out, en masse, after so many years of being told what to do and of having no freedom of movement whatsoever, we can better appreciate what it meant to them to have these powerful manifestations of God's leadership.

Angels in the Hebrew Bible/Old Testament frequently take on attributes of God, such as authority and wisdom, and the phrasing in these accounts has led scholars to make distinctions at times between what was simply an angel and what was some manifestation of God. However, none of this is very clear and we can only accept that, whatever these people or creatures were, they were acting in God's service and were to be obeyed as people were expected to obey God. When the term "angel of the Lord" is used in Scripture passages, sometimes that indicates the possibility that God was working quite directly through the angel, imbuing the messenger with qualities above and beyond those considered standard for an angel.

We might assume that an angel's accompanying presence is proof that we are on the right path. However, people have sometimes become aware of an angel's presence precisely because they were headed into danger and thus needed rescue or redirection. It seems, then, that angels walk with us regardless of our rightness or wrongness— and do so in fact because we make foolish choices and take the wrong path at times.

ANGELS GIVE US ENCOURAGEMENT AND INSTRUCTION

Then an angel of the Lord said to Philip, "Get up and go toward the south to the road that goes down from Jerusalem to Gaza." (Acts 8:26)

The Old Testament prophets frequently received marching orders from angels, whether in person or through dreams and visions. It's as if the angels were filling gaps of knowledge, supplying the information that was impossible to obtain otherwise. When a prophet existed out in the wilderness or among people who had wandered far from God, to what could he turn? During long periods in Israel's history, the written law of God was hidden away or simply forgotten. And wherever God was forgotten, the oral traditions about life with God were repeated less and less. Thus God's voice arrived in other ways. Righteous men and women received otherworldly visions. Or strangers appeared and spoke words that were too strange and true to be mere story and rumor.

In 1 Kings 18 in The Jewish Bible (chapter 19 in the Christian Old Testament), Elijah, prophet of God, challenges the priests of the false god called Baal. The King of Israel at this time is Ahab, who has married Jezebel, daughter of the King of Phoenicia. Jezebel has introduced worship of the Phoenician god Baal to Israel. Elijah sets up a contest between Baal and the God of Israel, saying to the people that they must choose whom they will worship. Elijah proposes that the priests of Baal prepare an altar and sacrifice, and he will do the same. They will see which God responds and burns up the sacrifice. After half a day of prayer and crying out and self-mutilation, the priests of Baal can elicit no response from their god. Elijah prepares a sacrifice, soaks it with water, prays a single prayer, and God sends down fire to lap up the water, the sacrifice, and the altar. This wins back the people of Israel, who put to death the priests of Baal. Unfortunately, the wicked Queen Jezebel is not intimidated and sends word to Elijah that he will be dead by the next day. So Elijah runs for his life.

[H]e . . . went a day's journey into the wilderness. He came to a broom bush and sat down under it, and prayed that he might die. "Enough!" he cried. "Now, O Lord, take my life, for I am no better than my fathers."
He lay down and fell asleep under a broom bush. Suddenly an angel touched him and said to him, "Arise and eat." He looked about; and there, beside his head, was a cake baked on hot stones and a jar of water! He ate and drank, and lay down again. The

angel of the LORD came a second time and touched him and said, "Arise and eat, or the journey will be too much for you." He arose and ate and drank; and with the strength from the meal he walked forty days and forty nights as far as the mountain of God at Horeb. There he went into a cave, and there he spent the night. (verses 4–9, Tanakh)

It is there at Mount Horeb, only after storms and whirlwinds and earthquakes and finally a soft, breezy silence, that Elijah is able to hear God's whisper and have a comprehensible conversation. After his stunning defeat of the prophets of Baal, he had run away, frightened and exhausted and, it appears, quite depressed. He told God, in essence, "Just kill me now." But God did not engage with Elijah directly; God sent an angel to feed the prophet and give him instructions for what would come next. It's as if Elijah was not truly ready to engage with God, and in the interim an angel stood by him and made sure he took care of himself and got back on the road. This story is told with such beauty and detail that perhaps we should receive it as a template. In our humanity, which is often weak, over-taxed, confused, angry, and in despair, we are unable to comprehend God's words to us, even if they are spoken audibly in our native tongue. We have to go through a process and be made ready for God's voice. It is often in this space that angels appear. They don't tell us theological secrets or answer our philosophical questions. They see to it that food and water materialize and that we get the road map. They become momentary companions, confirming that we're still going in the right direction. They help us get to where we can encounter God for ourselves.

And so angels appear to Abraham and assure him that what God promised will in fact come to pass; they appear to Moses with instructions for the grueling journey across the wilderness; they humor Gideon's endless doubts, affirming his being the leader God has called him to be.

During the earthly sojourn of Jesus, angels made significant appearances. They encouraged Jesus after his forty-day fast and subsequent temptation in the wilderness. The night before his death, during which he had to wrestle with his immediate future, he spent tormented hours at prayer in the Garden of Gethsemane. While his friends slept nearby, he had to decide one last time: Would he move forward into the awful reality of his impending trial, torture, and death? "Then an angel from heaven appeared to him and gave him strength. In his anguish he prayed more earnestly, and his sweat became like great drops of blood falling down on the ground" (Luke 22:43-44). It's significant that the angel came to encourage Jesus, after which Jesus still had to struggle and suffer and pray.

Jesus' life did not follow any script that people had been taught to expect, and it is no wonder that angels showed up at times to help Jesus' followers understand events as they unfolded. On the morning of his resurrection, when the women came to visit the tomb and found it empty, angels told them what had happened and instructed them to go tell the other disciples about the resurrection. When Jesus later ascended into heaven, angels were at hand (actually, up in the sky) to explain this as well. And in the chaotic days of the forming church, after Jesus' ascension, angels appeared to believers—we have stories from the lives of Paul, Philip, and others—to provide guidance and encouragement.

In the Qur'an, God tells the angels to "encourage the believers." Mohammad considered that angels assisted him along the way, from physical battles to heavenly journeys. And there is much Islamic tradition of Muslims' being helped by angelic visitors.

ANGELS APPEAR IN DREAMS AND VISIONS

One of the most famous angel dreams is that of the Jewish patriarch Jacob, when he was a young man fleeing the wrath of his brother Esau after having cheated Esau out of his birthright. As Jacob journeyed to another country, he slept one night on the ground and dreamed that he saw a ladder reaching up into heaven, with angels ascending and descending it. And the LORD stood beside him and told him what his destiny was to be. When Jacob awoke, he named the place Bethel, because he realized it was holy ground (Genesis 28).

Jacob dreamed of angels again years later, when he was working for his father-in-law Laban, who had cheated and deceived Jacob time and again. In a dream, an angel of the LORD told Jacob it was time to go back to his ancestors' country (Genesis 31). On the sojourn back, he encountered an angel once again, only this one was not in a dream but came as a man who wrestled with Jacob all night (Genesis 32).

The Christian tradition embraces these and other stories from the Hebrew Scriptures, and then adds some dream accounts of its own in the New Testament writings. The first significant dream we read about is Joseph's, after he learns that his bride-to-be is pregnant and claims that this has happened by the Holy Spirit. Not surprisingly, Joseph doesn't believe her but plans to end the engagement quietly and not bring attention to what he assumes is Mary's sin. Then an angel comes to Joseph in a dream and tells him that what Mary says is true, and that Joseph is to take her as his wife. It's interesting that although Mary is visited in person by the angel Gabriel, thereafter she must take direction from her husband's dreams. After the child Jesus is born, it is in Joseph's dream that an angel informs them of King Herod's mission to kill the child and that they must therefore flee to Egypt. And sometime later, Joseph dreams again and is told by an angel that it is now safe to return.

There's a fine line between dreams and visions, and angels appear in both. The Jewish prophet Zechariah records a rather involved vision in which a man under a myrtle tree interprets to Zechariah the scenes that unfold before him. Throughout his vision, he is aided by angels who illustrate and explain what is happening and what the vision means. This is similar to the various non-canonical dream-visions and journey-visions experienced through the centuries by Jewish, Christian, and Muslim mystics, in which angels guide the visionary on a journey through the seven heavens or to a future Jerusalem or to the throne of God. On such vision journeys the angels accompany the person and provide an explanation of what the person is witnessing.

ANGELS ASSIST IN HUMAN SPIRITUAL DEVELOPMENT

For the mission of the angels goes beyond enriching humans' knowledge of God; it also includes imparting to them energetic help toward their goal of spiritualization so that humans may thereby come to know God more easily.

Dumitru Staniloae, *The Experience of God*

Because angels were created, to exist with humanity and with God, the Church Fathers and Mothers have long understood that they have been involved from the very beginning with humanity's developing spirituality. Since early Judaism, it was believed that God communicated with humans through the angels, delivering not only specific, occasional messages but also the Law itself. Tradition has angels imparting the Ten Commandments; the New Testament writers refer to the law as having been given to us through the angels (Galatians 3:19; Hebrews

2:2; Acts 7:53). The theory was that, because no person could look upon God and live, from earliest times God had to use mediators when communicating with us. As the Jewish historian Josephus wrote: "It is from God, through angels, that we have learned the most beautiful of our doctrines and the most holy sections of our laws."

The role of guardian angels was also believed to be more than a physical guarding but also a guiding, almost as a human guardian or tutor would guide a young child into maturity. The early Christian church incorporated angels into the whole process of salvation as guides for us until the coming of Christ. The apostle Paul referred to the Law (that is, the laws of Moses given to the people of Israel) as a tutor for our souls until Christ would come, after which the law would not be our primary teacher. Enfolded in this understanding of the law was a belief that angels were also part of this early process of enlightenment and guidance. It was believed that, on an individual basis, guardian angels helped to care for and guide children into adulthood and further spiritual maturity.

This principle was applied to nations and peoples as well. Jean Danielou, S.J., in *The Angels and Their Mission According to the Fathers of the Church*, explains this application:

It is, in fact, a common doctrine in the whole of ancient tradition that God has entrusted the nations to His angels. This doctrine, which goes back to

Judaism, is echoed in the Greek translation of Deuteronomy 32:8. "When the Most High divided the nations, when he separated the sons of Adam, he appointed the bounds of people according to the number of the angels of God."

Danielou traces this belief in guiding angels for nations to Jewish apocalyptic literature, Philo of Alexandria, New Testament writers, Clement of Alexandria, and others. The Church Fathers believed that even pagan nations had retained some remnants of truth about God because of knowledge imparted by angels in ancient times. Unfortunately, human free will and the evil that resulted had prevented some societies from making much spiritual or moral headway, even with the help of angels. That is why Christ had to come, bringing completion of our knowledge and salvation for our souls.

If angels were given the task of guiding humanity in general, it follows that they were given a similar role in the church. Again, we find some of the most helpful material on this topic in the work of the Jesuit Danielou:

There is a very early tradition which sees angels placed at the head of Churches to establish and govern them. The foundation for this is in the first chapters of John's Apocalypse, where there is question of the angels of the seven Churches of Asia Minor. Origen can write in his turn: "One might say, following Scripture, that there are two bishops in each Church, one visible, and the other invisible, and that both are busied with the same task."

ANGELS DO BATTLE AGAINST EVIL

Given that the human universe is woven through with struggles for power, military warfare, and empire building, it's not surprising that angels show up on the battlefield, whether earthly or heavenly. In the Hebrew book of 2 Kings, chapter 6, the prophet Elisha is surrounded by the Aramean army.

> When an attendant of the man of God rose early and went outside, he saw a force, with horses and chariots, surrounding the town. "Alas, master, what shall we do?" his servant asked him. "Have no fear," he replied. "There are more on our side than on theirs." Then Elisha prayed: "LORD, open his eyes and let him see." And the LORD opened the servant's eyes and he saw the hills all around Elisha covered with horses and chariots of fire. [The Arameans] came down against him, and Elisha prayed to the Lord: Please strike this people with a blinding light." And He struck them with a blinding light, as Elisha had asked. (verses 15–18, Tanakh)

One psalm that is quoted often in treacherous situations is 34:7: "The angel of the LORD camps around those who fear Him and rescues them" (Tanakh).

Among the Dead Sea Scrolls was found a manuscript titled *The War of the Sons of Light Against the Sons of Darkness*. This text describes a strategy for battling the army of evil; the narrative seems to have a double meaning, referring to an actual physical battle in which the people (probably of the Jewish sect called the Essenes) must go to war, while also referring to a battle in which angels are present to fight for the good.

In the apocalyptic visions of St. John that come to us as the New Testament book of Revelation, angels are presented as warriors against the devil and the angels that join him. They deliver judgments in the form of plagues and are instrumental in overcoming the dragon, the beast—both metaphors for evil and the devil. The hosts of heaven are constant companions to the saints and martyrs. It is clear from this literature that angels are on the side of good and will go to battle for the sake of the multitudes that God is saving from evil and bringing into his presence.

St. Bernard of Clairvoux provides a passionate conclusion to this discussion:

Let us affectionately love His angels as one day our future coheirs; meanwhile, however, as counselors and defenders appointed by the Father and placed over us. Why should we fear under such guardians? Those who keep us in all our ways can neither be overcome nor be deceived, much less deceive. They are faithful; they are prudent; they are powerful; why do we tremble? Let us only follow them, let us remain close to them, and in the protection of the God of heaven let us abide.

PART TWO

A SHORT ENCYCLOPEDIA OF
Angels

A

Abaddon [Judaism, Christianity]: angel of destruction and of hell, or of the bottomless pit.

Abalim [Christianity]: another name for the order of angels called Thrones.

Abraham [Judaism, Christianity, Islam]: patriarch of the faith, the man to whom God made a covenant for all eternity and to whom God promised descendants more numerous than grains of sand. According to the book of Genesis, Abraham encountered angels twice. The first time, three strangers appeared to him at Mamre, where he lived. The one he spoke to was "the Lord," words that have been interpreted to be the angel of the Lord, that is, an angel standing in as a representative of God. The Lord's two companions were clearly angels. At this meeting the Lord tells the aged Abraham that Sarah will give birth to a son in a year. The Lord also tells Abraham that the three of them are traveling to Sodom to see if its evil is as bad as has been reported—and if so, Sodom will be destroyed. At this point, Abraham enters into his famous bargaining session with the Lord, or the Lord's angel, finally getting the stranger to agree that Sodom will be spared destruction if even ten righteous people are found there.

Abraham's second encounter with an angel happened when Abraham was about to follow God's command and sacrifice his only son Isaac on the altar. As he raised the knife, "the Lord's messenger called to him from heaven . . . 'Do not lay your hand on the boy. . . .'"

Abuliel [Judaism]: according to legend, the angel who takes human prayers—specifically, those of the Jews—to God.

Abyss, Angel of the [Christianity]: Found in the Book of Revelation, this angel oversees the great abyss into which evildoers are destroyed. Some legends identify this angel as Uriel.

Accuser [Judaism, Christianity]: name sometimes given to Satan, as the angel who accuses humanity before God's throne.

Accusing angel [Judaism, Christianity]: title sometimes given to an angel that becomes an adversary to a human, as in the book of Job. Satan is sometimes called "the Accuser" because, according to some Christian beliefs, he finds fault with human behavior and seeks to cripple people with guilt to prevent their repentance and restoration.

Adam [Judaism, Christianity, Islam]: the first man created, along with the first woman, Eve. They were placed in the Garden of Eden but were later cast out because they sinned—what is called the fall of humankind. According to Jewish legend, angels came to help the couple after the Fall, going so far as to give Adam secret wisdom (*Book of Raziel, Book of Adam*). In Islamic lore, Adam is connected with a pilgrimage to the holy city of Mecca, accompanied and/or helped by the angel Gabriel.

Af [Judaism]: in rabbinic lore, one of the five destroying angels, the angel of anger.

Agnes of Montepulciano [Christianity]: mystic of the late thirteenth century famous for her visions. Reportedly, an angel brought her communion.

Amulet: an object that can be worn or carried upon the body and on which pictures or words are inscribed to keep away evil. From ancient times, angel names have been used on amulets, including the amulets used within the magical/mystical traditions of Judaism and Christianity.

Anafiel [Judaism]: According to legend, Anafiel carried the patriarch Enoch to heaven. Anafiel is also said to have helped God in creation. In early traditions, Anafiel was even more prestigious than Metatron.

Anakim [Judaism, Christianity]: offspring of women and angels, referred to in the books of Genesis, Deuteronomy, and Joshua.

Ananchel [Judaism]: an angel that assisted Esther in gaining the king's favor. In rabbinic lore, the story of Esther (as found in the Book of Esther) is filled with angels that manipulate every circumstance so that the truth prevails and the Israelites are spared. In the biblical narrative, these angels are not mentioned.

Angel [Judaism, Christianity, Islam]: The concept of a spirit being that serves as mediator between deity and mortals has been present in cultures worldwide since earliest times. Judaism's beliefs about angels were influenced by the religions of Persia and Babylon; later Jewish and Christian beliefs were influenced by Greece and Rome. Islamic belief about angels is based somewhat on those of Judaism. Generally, people have believed that angels do the bidding of God, assist humans, and otherwise help in the various functions of the universe. Some doctrines—particularly those of Christianity—place angels in two categories: those that obey God and those that have rebelled against God—these rebels are sometimes referred to as demons. The faculties and functions of angels vary according to doctrine and tradition. They are considered more powerful and more knowledgeable than humans and are generally believed to be pure spirit, although they are able to take physical form.

Angelus [Christianity]: traditional Catholic prayer, recited morning, noon, and evening. This liturgy recalls the angel Gabriel's visit to Mary, and Mary's response. This communal prayer ends with these words: Lord, fill our hearts with your grace: / once, through the message of an angel / you revealed to us the incarnation of your Son; / now, through his suffering and death / lead us to the glory of his resurrection. / We ask this through Christ our Lord. / Amen.

Angelus occidentalis: a term that describes angels in general within the traditions of Zoroastrianism, Judaism, Christianity, and Islam.

Anne, St. [Christianity]: The mother of the Virgin Mary was married to Joachim, according to legend. She was unable to conceive until an angel appeared to her and told her to go to her husband, because she would have a child. She met her husband as he was coming in from the fields, and she did conceive and gave birth to Mary.

Annunciation, Angel of [Christianity]: title given to the Archangel Gabriel, because he was the angel sent to announce the birth of Jesus (and also the birth of John the Baptist).

Apollyon [Christianity]: the Greek name for the angel of the abyss (Revelation 9:11).

Apostate Angel [Christianity]: term for Satan used by Pope Gregory the Great.

Aputel [Judaism]: according to one of the earliest books of magic, the Key of Solomon, Aputel was a powerful angel whose name was on a plaque worn by priests when they entered the Holy of Holies. Supposedly, through the invocation of the name of this angel, the dead could be raised.

Aravot [Judaism]: highest heavenly realm.

Arch Fiend [general]: one of the many titles for Satan.

Archangels [Judaism, Christianity, Islam]: They comprise the eighth choir of the heavenly hosts, the ninth (and those closest to earthly matters) being angels. In Revelation 8:2, seven of them stand before God; thus Christians have considered that there are seven Archangels, who command the angels under them. In the Bible we find Michael, Gabriel, and Raphael; tradition names the remaining four as Uriel, Chamael, Jophiel, and Zadkiel.

Jewish tradition names Michael, Gabriel, Raphael, and Uriel as the four Archangels that stand before God's presence. Depending on the source, there are other Archangels, numbering from seven to ten.

Islam has four Archangels: Michael, Gabriel, Israfil, and Izra'il. They are considered to be angels that stay close to God's presence, and one classification for them is Qaribiyyun, or "Cherubim."

Archons [Judaism, Christianity]: angels in charge of nations; sometimes referred to as princes.

Arelim [Judaism]: an order of angels named in some literature.

Ark of the Covenant [Judaism, Christianity]: According to the description in Exodus 25 of the Ark of the Covenant, two images of Cherubim were made of beaten gold and placed on the top piece. The tablets on which the commandments were written were placed inside the ark. Moses was instructed that the space between the two cherubim was where God would meet him to give instruction. Although these cherubim were made of gold, it would appear that they represented God's throne in heaven, which is surrounded by angels. In Jewish legend, these two angels are sometimes named as Zarall and Jael, and sometimes the great angel Sandalphon is identified with the Ark.

Armageddon [Christianity]: the location of the final war between God and the heavenly hosts and Satan and the demons of hell. This story is told in the book of Revelation. Armageddon figures significantly into the end-time theology that developed in some Protestant circles from the mid-1800s. The term "Armageddon" has occurred in various popular films and stories in which a climactic battle between good and evil is fought.

Asaph [Judaism, Christianity]: named as the author of Psalms 50, and 73–83. Some legends identify Asaph as an angel.

Ascension [Judaism, Christianity, Islam]: generally refers to the soul of a person rising up into heaven after that person's death. In all three faiths, angels are said to escort the soul to heaven (or hell, as the case may be). Sometimes ascension does not necessarily require death, as in the Prophet Mohammad's Night Journey, when the Archangel Jibril (Gabriel) took him to Jerusalem and then to heaven and back. And in the New Testament, the resurrected Christ ascended into heaven before many witnesses, from the Mount of Olives. While they were watching, "suddenly two men in white robes stood by them. They said, 'Men of Galilee, why do you stand looking up toward heaven? This Jesus, who has been taken up from you into heaven, will come in the same way . . .'" (Acts 1:10-11).

Asmodeus [Judaism, Christianity]: This angel first appeared in Persian legends. In the Old Testament book of Tobit, Asmodeus is the demon that has killed seven husbands in a row, each on his wedding night before the marriage can be consummated. They were all husbands of the young Sarah, daughter of Raguel. The angel Raphael tells Tobias how to get rid of the demon. On the night of Tobias' marriage to Sarah, he puts a fish heart and liver on the burning incense in the room, and this sends Asmodeus fleeing to Egypt, where the angel Raphael captures and binds the demon.

Aureole: the light that encircles an angel or members of the Godhead or holy persons (a halo encircles only the head).

Authorities [Christianity]: one of the classes of angels in the heavenly hierarchy.

Avenging angels [Judaism, Christianity]: angels sent by God to avenge evil on earth or to bring judgment. Although these angels bring bad circumstances to people, they serve the judgment of God and are in fact angels and not demons.

Azazel [Judaism]: Legend has it that two angels, Azazel and Shemhazai, went down to earth to prove to God that they could resist evil. However, they lusted after human women and had sex with them. One version of this legend says that their offspring were the Nefilim. Some legends say that Shemhazai repented but that Azazel never did and has been left suspended in a canyon in the wilderness. Azazel was also connected to folklore surrounding the scapegoat upon which the sins of the people were transferred on the Day of Atonement.

Azrael [Judaism, Islam]: angel of death.

Baby angels [Christianity]: sometimes called cherubs or putti. They have often appeared accompanying the Virgin Mary in apparitions of her.

Balaam [Christianity]: He was a prophet whom Balak, the king of Moab, sought out for help. Balak wanted Balaam to curse the Israelites, thus giving the Moabites victory over them. As God's prophet, Balaam knew better than to curse God's chosen people, and he sent this message to Balak. However, after some persuading on the part of Balak, Balaam decided to go talk with him and set out on his donkey. God put an angel on the pathway, armed with a sword, to prevent this journey, but Balaam didn't see the angel. The donkey did, however, and three different times the animal went off the path or stopped altogether, although Balaam beat her each time she did. At that point, God enabled the donkey to speak, and she asked Balaam why he was beating her, when she had served him for so long and had never acted this way before. Then God opened Balaam's eyes, and he saw the angel and understood that the donkey had probably saved his life. (See Numbers 22.)

Balm: This symbol has often been identified with the Archangel Raphael, who is said to be the angel of healing. This identification of Raphael comes from the account of his healing powers in the Book of Tobit.

Baruch [Judaism]: four apocryphal books have been attributed to Baruch, all of which contain much information about angels: *Apocalypse of Baruch, Book of Baruch, The Greek Apocalypse of Baruch,* and *The Rest of the Words of Baruch.*

Baruchiel [Judaism, Christianity]: Baruchiel is not named in any canon of Scripture but in some legends is identified as an Archangel.

Beelzebub [Judaism, Christianity]: means "lord of the flies." Named in the kabbalist writings as chief of the underworld. In the Gospels of Matthew (12), Mark (3), and Luke (11), he is called the ruler of demons.

Behemoth [Judaism, Christianity]: in Jewish lore is a monster; in Christian legend is a demon.

Bel and the Dragon [Judaism, Christianity]: In this legend, Daniel was thrown into the lions' den because he killed the dragon worshiped by the Babylonians. He was there for seven days, and although the lions were usually well fed, Daniel's captors withheld food so the lions would eat Daniel. On day six, an angel of the Lord went to a prophet named Habakkuk, off in Judea, who was making stew to take out to the harvesters. The angel said, "Take the meal you are carrying to Babylon and give it to Daniel in the lion pit," to which Habakkuk said innocently, "I have not even seen Babylon, and know nothing about this pit." So the angel yanked up Habakkuk by his hair and carried him to Babylon and set him on the edge of the lion pit. Habakkuk called down to Daniel, saying that his meal was ready, and Daniel quite graciously ate it. The angel quickly dispatched Habakkuk back to Judea. Of course, when the king discovered, on day seven, that Daniel was unharmed, he decided to worship Daniel's god after all. Those who had plotted Daniel's death were thrown into the lion pit, and the lions devoured them right away.

Belial [Christianity]: St. Paul equates Belial with Satan in 2 Corinthians 6:15.

Beliar [Judaism, Christianity]: another name for Belial. Beliar shows up in apocryphal literature, usually as a demon.

Bene Elohim [Judaism, Christianity]: In some Jewish angelic hierarchies, these angels belong to the order of

Thrones. They have also been identified as the angelic beings who had sex with women in Genesis 2.

Bethesda, pool of [Christianity]: according to some versions of John's Gospel, chapter 5, this pool at one of Jerusalem's gates was said to be visited periodically by an angel who stirred its waters; when this happened, the waters had healing power. Some traditions name Raphael as the angel who visited this pool.

Blinded Angel [Christianity]: Pope John Paul II used this term for Satan.

Bochim [Judaism, Christianity]: place where an angel of the Lord appeared to the Israelites to upbraid them for not tearing down pagan altars, as they had been instructed (Judges 2).
Book of Jubilees [Judaism]: a pseudepigraphical text, which has various references to angels.

Book of Mormon: said to be the revelation delivered to Joseph Smith by the angel Moroni.

Bottomless pit [Judaism, Christianity]: term used for hell or the place of the dead, whose ruler is the devil.

Bottomless pit, Angel of the [Christianity]: same as angel of the abyss, as in Revelation 20.

Brilliant Ones [Christianity]: another name for the class of angels called Virtues.

Burning bush [Judaism, Christianity]: When Moses was a shepherd in Midian, he saw one day on Mt. Horeb a bush that was on fire but was not consumed. "There the angel of the LORD appeared to him in a flame of fire out of a bush" (Exodus 3:2). God spoke out of the bush and commissioned Moses to lead the Israelites out of Egypt. This is one of several instances where the forms "angel of the LORD" and "the LORD" are used interchangeably.

Captain of the host of the Lord [Judaism, Christianity]: the angel who appeared to Joshua and instructed him on how to capture Jericho.

Celestial bodies [Christianity]: in 1 Corinthians 15:40, Paul made this reference to angels.

Celestial choir [Christianity]: term for angels.

Celestial orders [Christianity]: a term for the various categories of angels.

Cerviel [Judaism]: according to legend, it was Cerviel who helped the boy David defeat the giant Goliath.

Chamuel [Christianity]: sometimes spelled Camael; listed by some sources as one of the seven Archangels who stand before God's throne. This angel shows up in various legends, named in some as the angel who wrestled with Jacob and in others as one of the angels that ministered to Christ in the Garden of Gethsemane.

Chashmalim [Judaism, Christianity]: otherworldly creatures described in Ezekiel 1:5.

Chayot [Judaism, Christianity]: heavenly beings described in Ezekiel 1:5–14. They each had four wings and four faces.

Cherub [Christianity]: baby angel, or putti. The name is taken from Psalm 18:10: "He rode on a cherub, and flew; / he came swiftly upon the wings of the wind."

Cherubim [Judaism, Christianity, Islam]: word meaning "mighty ones"; one of the higher orders of angels in Judaism, the second highest order of angels in the traditional Christian hierarchy. In Islam as well they are an order of angels who remain near God's throne singing praises.

Children [Christianity]: In Matthew's Gospel, Jesus says, "Take care that you do not despise one of these little ones; for, I tell you, in heaven their angels continually see the face of my Father in heaven" (18:10). This verse is one basis for the Christian belief in guardian angels.

Companion angel: another term for guardian angel.

Conductor of souls [Judaism, Christianity]: an angel that takes mortal souls into the spiritual realm; another name for this is psychepomp.

Confusion, angels of [Judaism]: according to lore, there are seven, who acted in the court of Ahasuerus (story of Esther) and possibly at the Tower of Babel.

Cornelius [Christianity]: He was a gentile centurion of Caesarea, "a devout man who feared God" who had a vision one afternoon of an angel who instructed him to contact Simon Peter in Joppa. Cornelius sent some men to find Peter, and while they were on the journey, Peter, who was Jewish, experienced a vision in which he was told, "What God has made clean, you must not call profane." The meaning of this became clear when Cornelius' messengers showed up at Peter's door. Peter heeded God's message from the dream and went to Cornelius' home to teach him about Jesus. This was a radical step for a Jew, and it began to open the minds of Jesus' followers, who were primarily Jewish, to see other people as welcome to the family of God.

Countenance, angel(s) of [Judaism]: an angel or angels that were visible manifestations of God. It is not clear whether this term describes a specific order of angels or individual angels (Metatron has been named such) that are sometimes given that function.

Cupid: in Roman mythology, the god of love, also called Amor. Cupid had wings, and legends about this god likely merged to some extent with Judeo-Christian lore about winged messengers called angels.

Daimon (or daemon): a Greek version of angel, believed to be a spirit that worked between the human and the divine. Served many of the same functions that have been attributed to angels—as guardians and protectors and those who encouraged people and offered them information or wisdom.

Daniel, book of [Judaism, Christianity]: the book of Daniel names the two Archangels Gabriel (Daniel 8:15–17) and Michael (Daniel 10:12–14). Also, in this book, angels rescue Daniel's companions, appearing with them in the fiery furnace, from which all come out unhurt, and the angels later rescue Daniel from the lion pit. The book of Daniel was the first Judaic literature that began to develop the concepts of individual angels and angelic hierarchies.

Daniel, prophet [Judaism, Christianity]: He was a Hebrew exile in Babylon to whom God gave the ability to interpret dreams of King Nebuchadnezzar. Later, under King Darius, Daniel was thrown into the lions' den for a trumped-up charge of insubordination. But God sent an angel and closed the lions' mouths so that Daniel survived. Later, the angel Gabriel came to Daniel to give him special understanding of the events to come. And "a man clothed in linen, with a belt of gold from Uphaz around his waist," appeared to Daniel to strengthen and encourage him. (See the Book of Daniel, chapters 9 and 10.)

Dark angel(s) [Judaism, Christianity]: term used for Satan, demons. Some sources name the dark angel as the one who wrestled with Jacob.

Darkness, angel of [Judaism, Christianity, Islam]: another term for Satan, or the devil.

Dead Sea Scrolls [Judaism, Christianity]: Discovered in 1947, they date from the first century and were produced by the Qumran community, a Jewish sect. These writings give a significant place to angels, and in them we find the angel of darkness, also known as Belial and the angel of truth, who is Michael. Their respective armies are the sons of darkness and the sons of light.

Death, angel of [Judaism, Christianity, Islam]: this term generally has two meanings. Sometimes it is synonymous with the angel of destruction, who brings death to people as an act of God's judgment against them, such as the angel who destroyed tens of thousand of Israel's enemies at once. But the angel of death is also known as the angel who comes to accompany mortals when they die and take them to the spiritual realm. Some traditions name this angel as Samael. In Islam, Azrael is the angel of death.

Demon [Judaism, Christianity, Islam]: generally believed to be one of the angels who fell from heaven by rebelling against God. One Jewish legend says that demons are spirits who were not paired with bodies because the sixth day of creation ended before God could create bodies for them.

Deputy angels [Judaism]: In magical practice of Jewish lore, a deputy angel is one that can be conjured by a magician in order to bring help or service; generally believed to be evil.

Destroying angel(s) [Judaism]: In rabbinic lore, there are five destroying angels: Af, Hemah, Ketzeph, Hashmed, and Hashbeth. Individual destroying angels appear in various legends, often involving the patriarchs.

Destruction, angels of [Judaism, Christianity, Islam]: angels sent to inflict punishment upon the wicked on earth and upon the damned in hell. Two of these angels destroyed Sodom and Gomorrah (Genesis 19), and a single angel wiped out 70,000 in 1 Chronicles 21:14 and the Assyrian army in 2 Kings 19:35.

Devil [Judaism, Christianity]: Satan or Lucifer, God's adversary.

Dionysius the Areopagite [Christianity]: a convert of the apostle Paul. He is credited with writing four important works on spirituality: *The Celestial Hierarchies, The Divine Names, The Ecclesiastical Hierarchy,* and *The Mystical Theology.* In *The Celestial Hierarchies,* he developed an angelology that gained the respect of early leaders in the Church, including Pope Gregory the Great and Thomas Aquinas. Dionysius' angelic hierarchy became the standard in Christianity.

However, most scholars today do not think that these writings could have come from the Dionysius of Paul's time but were written, probably in the sixth century, by someone else using Dionysius' name. In many reference works, Dionysius the Areopagite is called Pseudo-Dionysius the Areopagite.

Divine Presence, Angels of [Judaism, Christianity]: angels who stand before God. They number from four to seven, and the lists of their names vary.

Dominations [Christianity]: fourth order of angels in the hierarchy of Dionysius. According to tradition, they help govern the universe, including the lower orders of angels.

Dragon [Christianity]: one term used for Satan in the book of Revelation.

Dragon slayer [Christianity]: Michael the Archangel, so titled because he battles the dragon (Satan) in Revelation.

Dumiel [Judaism]: in rabbinic lore this angel of the divine silence was one of the two that guarded the gate to the sixth heaven.

Dumah [Judaism]: According to lore, Dumah was the angel prince in charge of Egypt. When Dumah heard that God would judge the gods of Egypt and free the Israelites from Egyptian bondage, Dumah opposed Moses. Some legends claim that he tried to frighten the Israelites as they left Egypt. Because of his rebellion, Dumah was removed as prince of Egypt and sent to command the angels of destruction, and has since been known as the ruler of Gehenna, the realm of the dead.

Dybbuk [Judaism]: the soul of a dead person who possesses the body of a living person—not to be confused with a demon.

Eden, Garden of [Judaism, Christianity, Islam]: the earthly paradise in which Adam and Eve were placed, invited to eat of any tree of the garden except one: the tree of the knowledge of good and evil. When Adam and Eve disobeyed and ate of that tree's fruit, God cast them out of the garden. And God posted at the gate of the garden two Cherubim, to guard the tree of life. In Jewish lore, these two angels are Jetatron or Jophiel.

Elders [Christianity]: John's vision in Revelation 4 describes twenty-four beings on thrones that surround God's throne; many scholars believe that these beings are angels, possibly that represent the twelve tribes of Israel and the twelve apostles.

Elementals: according to magic lore, spirit beings said to inhabit the four elements of life: earth, water, fire, and air. Some elementals were good and some were evil. They were not considered angels per se, more in the realm of the Arabic jinn, which inhabited objects and places and could be good or evil.

Elijah [Judaism, Christianity, Islam]: a prophet famous for his defeat of the prophets of Baal on Mt. Carmel. After Elijah displayed God's power, the evil Jezebel swore to Elijah that she would have his life, and so he fled, ending up in the desert, in a cave. There he prayed for death and then fell asleep, exhausted. He was awakened by an angel who told him to get up and eat—providing food for him. Elijah ate and then fell asleep again, and the angel woke him a second time, urging him to eat, "otherwise the journey will be too much for you" (1 Kings 19:7).

In Jewish lore, Elijah becomes an angel upon being carried off to heaven. He is the great Sandolphon, twin of Metatron, who is said to be the former patriarch Enoch. In one Jewish prayer, Elijah is the "Angel of the Covenant." He is said to record the deeds of all the living.

Elisha [Judaism, Christianity]: The prophet who succeeded Elijah. When the Aramean forces surrounded Elisha to kill him, his assistant panicked, but Elisha asked the Lord to open the young man's eyes, and he saw "the mountain was full of horses and chariots of fire all around Elisha" (2 Kings 6:17). This image of heaven's army has figured into art and folklore ever since.

Elohim [Judaism]: one term used for angels; in some sources it refers to a specific order of angels.

Enoch [Judaism, Christianity]: Hebrew patriarch, best known as the one who did not experience a natural death but simply walked with God and then "was no more" (Genesis 5:24). In Jewish lore, he was taken by an angel through the seven heavens, and once in God's presence was transformed into the great angel Metatron. Legend attributes to him the three Books of Enoch. Alan F. Segal (*Life after Death: A History of the Afterlife in Western Tradition*) suspects that the Enoch stories in Genesis and the Pseudepigraphica grew out of the Mesopotamian legends of wise men who traveled to heaven.

Enoch, Books of [Judaism]: three pseudepigraphical works attributed to the patriarch Enoch. They were actually composed at different periods and by numerous authors. The three books of Enoch comprise some of the most significant vision literature of early Jewish mysticism and include stories of heavenly journeys and encounters with angels. Some scholars consider the books of Enoch as links between the prophecies in the book of Daniel and the writings of the Essenes, or the Qumran community. Some of these writings were well known and cited by Christians such as Origen and Clement of Alexandria.

Esdras (or Ezdras), book of [Judaism, Christianity]: apocryphal book telling the story, in first person, of the prophet Ezra. He relates various visions he was given and their interpretation by the angel Uriel.

Essenes [Judaism]: a Jewish community/sect existing during the first century that followed strict religious practices. They were also possibly the first sect in Judaism to develop a system of angelology. The Dead Sea Scrolls are of Essene origin, and we read about angels and demons especially in two of their documents, *The War of the Sons of Light Against the Sons of Darkness* and *The Manual of Discipline*.

Ethnarchs [Judaism, Christianity]: another name for archons, or angels who serve as guardians of nations or regions.
Evening Star: term sometimes referring to Lucifer, or Satan.

Ezekiel [Judaism, Christianity]: a prophet among the exiles in Babylon between 593 and 571 BCE; his elaborate visions have been the fodder of apocalyptic lore as well as speculation about Unidentified Flying Objects. Here is an opening description of creatures in his first vision: "They were of human form. Each had four faces, and each of them had four wings. Their legs were straight, and the soles of their feet were like the sole of a calf's foot; and they sparkled like burnished bronze. Under their wings on their four sides they had human hands. And the four had their faces and their wings thus: their wings touched one another; each of them moved straight ahead, without turning as they moved. As for the appearance of their faces: the four had the face of a human being, the face of a lion on the right side, the face of an ox on the left side, and the face of an eagle; such were their faces. Their wings were spread out above; each creature had two wings, each of which touched the wing of another, while two covered their bodies. Each moved straight ahead; wherever the spirit would go, they went, without turning as they went" (Ezekiel 1:5–12).

Face, angels of the [Judaism]: those select angels who behold God's face. Sources give different numbers, from four to twelve. They are also called angels of the presence.

Fallen angels [Judaism, Christianity, Islam]: those angels who rebelled against God in one way or another and thus were cast out of heaven (or according to some lore left heaven voluntarily, which led to their status of "fallen").

Various versions of angelic disobedience and subsequent punishment are presented in all three of the Abrahamic traditions, and several of them are similar to one another.

Generally, angelic disobedience was related to how the angels responded to God's creation of, or honor given to, humanity. And the common belief about fallen angels (called demons in Christian theology) is that they continue to harass human beings and attempt to lead to human sorrow and destruction.

Feast of the Guardian Angels [Christianity]: a Catholic holiday (October 2) to celebrate the angels. Whereas each Archangel once had a feast day, now only Michael has his own feast, which is called Michaelmas (September 29).

Fiery furnace [Judaism, Christianity]: in Babylon, around the sixth century BCE, when three young Hebrew exiles refused to worship a golden statue, King Nebuchadnezzar had them thrown into a huge furnace. But the king saw three, not four, men walking around in the flames unhurt. This fourth man has been believed to be an angel.

Fire [Judaism, Christianity, Islam]: Angels have often been connected with fire. According to Jewish lore, angels were made from pure fire. Some legends talk of a heavenly river of fire, Rigyon, from which angels emerge daily and into which they are consumed. In Islamic lore, the jinn—a spiritual form lower than the angels—are made from smokeless fire. In some literature angels are called flames.

Food of angels [Judaism]: tradition names manna as this food, and maintains that it is created in the third sphere of the heavens, which is called "The Clouds."

Forces [Christianity]: one term used by St. John of Damascus for the angelic order of Virtues or Powers.

Four angels [Judaism, Christianity, Islam]: Some Jewish traditions name four angels who stand in God's presence (others number them at seven or twelve). The significance of four angels in Christianity lies mainly in the Book of Revelation, chapter 7, where four angels stand at four corners of the earth holding back the four winds. Islam cites four angels that bear up God's throne. The four most commonly named angels in Judaism and Christianity are Michael, Gabriel, Raphael, and Uriel.

Frances of Rome [Christianity]: mystic of late fourteenth and early fifteenth centuries who was guided the last twenty-three years of her life by her guardian angel, who was visible to her but no one else. Frances was considered responsible for numerous miraculous healings, which she attributed to the angel. Her last words: "The angel has finished his work. He is beckoning me to follow."

Francis of Assisi [Christianity]: the first saint to have received the stigmata—that is, wounds similar to those of the crucified Christ appeared on Francis's body. This happened during the saint's vision on Mt. Alverna. Francis saw what appeared to be a flaming Seraph with six wings coming down from heaven. As it came closer, Francis could see that the angel was also crucified. This sight caused within Francis great pain but also overwhelming, passionate love for Christ. When the vision was gone, Francis bore the wounds in his hands, feet, and side.

Gabriel [Judaism, Christianity, Islam]: one of the highest-ranking angels. In various myths and theologies Gabriel is considered one of the four angels that stand in God's presence as well as one of the seven Archangels. Gabriel is known as the angel of the annunciation because he announced to the Virgin Mary the coming birth of her son, Jesus. Gabriel makes announcements in other Bible narratives, to the prophet Daniel and to the priest Zechariah. In Jewish lore Gabriel, whose name means "God is my strength," is the angel who gives us courage and strength. In some legends he is also the prince of fire.

In Islam, Gabriel (pronounced "Jibril") was the angel who delivered the Qur'an to the prophet Mohammad and appeared to him at various times. One of the most important of these events was the Night Journey, whereby Gabriel escorted Muhammad to Jerusalem to pray with the prophets, among them Abraham, Moses, and Jesus. From Jerusalem Gabriel carried him up to heaven, where

Muhammad received special instructions from God before returning to earth. Sometimes Jibril is referred to in the Qur'an as the holy spirit.

Gabriel is named in many legends of all three traditions.

Gehenna [Judaism, Christianity, Islam]: another name for hell—where the souls of evil people are taken for punishment. Originally, Gehenna was a valley near Jerusalem where former inhabitants had sacrificed children to their god Moloch; it became a place for burning the bodies of people who were not allowed proper burial.

Gemma Galgani [Christianity]: mystic of late nineteenth century who, along with receiving the stigmata (physical wounds of Christ) claimed to see her guardian angel regularly. The angel would talk with her about the suffering and death of Christ.

Gethsemane, Garden of [Christianity]: a garden near the Mount of Olives, east of Jerusalem. It was here that Jesus prayed in great agony before he was arrested and then put to death. During this long night, an angel came from heaven to give him strength (Luke 22:43).

Giants [Judaism, Christianity]: Genesis 6 mentioned a race of giants who were the offspring of fallen angels and human women, a theme of several legends. One name for this hybrid race is Nefilim.

Gideon [Judaism, Christianity]: In Orpah, a young man named Gideon was threshing wheat in the winepress so the Midianites wouldn't detect him. As told in Judges 6, there in the winepress "The angel of the LORD appeared to him and said to him, 'The LORD is with you, you mighty warrior.'" The boy had spunk, because he hardly missed a beat: "But sir, if the LORD is with us, why then has all this happened to us? And where are all his wonderful deeds that our ancestors recounted to us, saying, 'Did not the LORD bring us up from Egypt?' But now the LORD has cast us off, and given us into the hand of Midian." The angel said that he, Gideon, would rescue Israel from the power of Midian, and Gideon reminded the stranger that not only was his father's tribe the least of all in Israel, but he was the least of his father's sons. The angel insisted that Gideon would crush their enemies. So Gideon said, in essence, "Excuse me, but your word isn't enough; let me prepare a sacrifice for you." So Gideon brought back bread and meat and broth, set it there, and the angel touched the food with the tip of his staff, whereupon fire sprang up and consumed the sacrifice, and the angel vanished. At that point, Gideon assumed he would die, because he had, after all, just seen the angel of the Lord. But the Lord assured him he would not die.

Still, this wasn't enough for Gideon—he put God to several other tests after that, but finally relinquished and became the warrior God called him to be. We have to imagine the humor of the angel's initial address, "mighty warrior," to this boy who was so unsure of himself and not terribly confident in God either.

God of this age [Christianity]: term used for Satan in 2 Corinthians 4 (KJV). In other versions it is "god of this world."

Golden tablets [Christianity]: according to the Mormon faith, the angel Moroni led Joseph Smith to golden tablets upon which were engraved writings that developed into the Book of Mormon.

Gomorrah [Judaism, Christianity]: sister city of Sodom, which was destroyed by two angels for its great evil (Genesis 19).

Good Inclination [Judaism]: tradition claims that God created an Evil Inclination and a Good Inclination, to which each person has opportunity to respond. Some legends say that the two guardian angels that watch over each person represent the two inclinations.

Grim Reaper: a popular term for the angel of death.

Guardian angel [Judaism, Christianity, Islam]: angel assigned to watch over a specific person. Christians have held the general belief that each person has a guardian (based upon Jesus' comment in Matthew 18:10). Islamic tradition holds that each person has two guardians (see

Hafazah). Jewish tradition assigns to each person anywhere from two to 11,000 guardian angels.

In Judaism and Christianity, there are also angel guardians over nations.

ℋ

Hades [Judaism, Christianity]: place of the dead, watched over by an angel or angels.

Hafazah [Islam]: guardian angels. Each person has two for day and two for night—and people are in the most danger at dawn or sunset, when the guard is changed. Not only do hafazah protect humans, they record every deed in books that will be opened on the Day of Judgment. These two angels are sometimes called recorder angels.

Hagar [Judaism, Christianity, Islam]: the handmaid of Sarah, by whom Abraham fathered Ishmael. Hagar fled twice, in Genesis 16 and 21, and the first time was instructed by an angel to return, and the second time an angel provided sustenance in the wilderness and promised God's provision for Hagar and her son.

Halo: light encircling the head of a holy person or an angel. Depictions of the halo pre-date Christianity.

Hanuel, or Haniel [Judaism, Christianity]: according to some traditions, one of the seven Archangels.

Harp: one of the symbols associated with angels, probably because they are said to sing praises to God.

Harut and Marut [Islam]: When the angels protested God's favor toward human beings, God said that if the angels were sensual creatures as humans were, the angels, too, would sin. As a test, the angels chose two of their number, Harut and Marut, two of the most humble angels, to go to earth with sensual traits. Eventually, Harut and Marut committed all the sins human beings were guilty of. Ever since, the angels have asked God's forgiveness for humankind.

Hashbeth [Judaism]: in rabbinic lore, one of the five destroying angels, the angel of Annihilation.

Hashmed [Judaism]: in rabbinic lore, one of the five destroying angels, the angel of Destruction.

Hayyot [Judaism]: order of angels that bear up God's throne, mentioned in Ezekiel 1.

Heavenly Academy [Judaism]: term used in the Zohar for a group of angels who judge humans when they arrive in heaven.

Heavenly host [Judaism, Christianity]: general term for angels.

Hekhalot [Judaism]: Hebrew word meaning palaces. A branch of mysticism arose in early Judaism that involved journeys to the various palaces of heaven.

Hell [Judaism, Christianity]: the place where the wicked are sent after the final judgment. In some Jewish legends Uriel is in charge of hell; Christian tradition holds that Satan rules hell; and in Islam Malik is named as the angel in charge of hell.

Hemah [Judaism]: in rabbinic lore, one of the five destroying angels, the angel of wrath.

Hermes: in Greek mythology, Hermes was a divine messenger with wings who carried mortal souls to Hades. This is another example of winged angel-like beings appearing in cultures outside Judaism. The Greek mythology probably strengthened the Judeo-Christian concept of winged messengers.

Herod [Christianity]: Jewish king in Acts 12 who was struck dead by an angel of the Lord because he glorified himself rather than God.

Holy beasts [Judaism]: term used in the Talmud for Cherubim.

Holy House of Loreto [Christianity]: house in which the Virgin Mary was supposedly born and where she was visited by the angel Gabriel when he announced to her the coming birth of her son Jesus. These beliefs would make it extraordinary enough, but Christians have believed for centuries that angels carried this house from Nazareth and placed it in the town of Tersato, Italy, in 1291, then moved it several times again until it rested finally in the town of Loreto, near the sea, where it still stands. This belief has become established in the Catholic tradition and honored by numerous popes and saints. It's been reported that the house does not rest on any foundation and that the materials from which it is made are unlike any in the area and are in fact similar to materials found in Nazareth.

Holy Ones [Judaism]: a traditional term for angels.

Holy Sefiroth [Judaism]: Kabbalist concept of specific aspects and manifestations of God's essence. Some traditions have assigned an Archangel to each of these.

Hosts [Judaism, Christianity]: a traditional term for angels.

Humans and angels [Judaism, Christianity, Islam]: Angels are generally believed to act as agents of God in the interest of humanity. In all three traditions there exist certain beliefs that it is possible for humans to evolve spiritually to the point that they can become like angels. Some of the mystical traditions of Judaism claim that the great patriarchs were transformed into angels when they entered heaven. In Catholic tradition, the Virgin Mary is believed to have been crowned Queen of the Angels, or Queen of Heaven, upon her assumption into heaven.

7

Iblis [Islam]: the angel that refused to bow down and worship the newly created Adam per God's instruction. Some sources identify Iblis (Satan, or devil) as chief of the jinn, which are not fallen angels but a spirit form lower than the angels. Iblis tempted Adam and Eve in the Garden of Eden. The devil continues to tempt humans and try to mislead them.

Illumination [Judaism, Christianity]: Angels act as intermediaries between God and humanity, inspiring us toward spiritual maturity, illumining human souls in preparation for their ultimate communion with God. Early Jewish and Christian tradition attributes to the angels this task of helping humans along their spiritual pathway of enlightenment, assisting our souls in their development and their eventual dwelling in God's presence with the angels.

Incubi [Christianity]: one term used by some of the early Church Fathers for fallen angels who had sex with human women.

Inspiration [Judaism, Christianity, Islam]: Angels can inspire humans toward good by impressing upon us good thoughts and inclinations. In the same way, fallen angels (demons) work to inspire us toward evil.

Intelligences [Christianity, Islam]: a term used for angels by some mystics and scholars, who considered angels pure intelligences having no physical being. In this way they are above humans in the cosmos, because humans are part of the material world.

Intercession by angels [Judaism, Christianity, Islam]: At times, angels have been known to pray to God on behalf of humankind. In the Islamic legend of Harut and Marut, ever since these two angels sinned as humans did, they have asked God's forgiveness for humanity's sins. In various Jewish legends, angels intercede for the people of Israel, and they mourn when God sends judgment upon them. In the book of Tobit, the Archangel Raphael says to Tobit: "[Wh]en you and Sarah prayed, it was I who brought and read the record of your prayer before the glory of the Lord" (Tobit 12:12).

Iophiel [Judaism]: according to lore, one of the Archangels; some sources name Iophiel as the angel of the Torah.

Irinim [Judaism]: sometimes called Watchers, a high order of angels who stand around God and argue all cases before him.

Isaac [Judaism, Christianity]: son of the patriarch Abraham. Isaac's birth was announced by three angels who visited Abraham. Years later, when God put Abraham to the test by requiring that he offer his son as a burnt sacrifice, Abraham was about to kill Isaac when God sent an angel to prevent him.

Isaiah [Judaism, Christianity]: the prophet whose vision of angels (Isaiah 6) is one of the most celebrated. He saw angels surrounding God's throne. One of them, a Seraph, carried a live coal to touch Isaiah's lips and thus purify him for God's service.

Israfel [Islam]: This angel sings God's praises in a thousand languages. Israfel will blow the trumpet on the Last Day and is sometimes called the angel of Resurrection and the angel of the Last Judgment.

Izra'il [Islam]: angel of death.

J

Jabarut [Islam]: more precisely, 'alam al-jabarut, meaning "world of the angels." This is the third level of existence in the Muslim ideology of the Five Divine Presences, being one level above that of the jinn and two levels above human existence.

Jacob [Judaism, Christianity, Islam]: The wily son of
Isaac, he cheated his brother Esau out of a birthright and
then fled for his life. He ended up with his uncle Laban in
Haran. On his journey, he settled down for the night with
a rock for a pillow. He had a dream that night of a ladder
that extended from the ground to heaven, and angels of
God were ascending and descending it (Genesis 28:12).
God spoke to Jacob in this dream, promising him a good
future. Upon waking, Jacob realized that he had slept on
holy ground; he used his stone pillow to make an altar,
poured oil over it, and named the place Bethel.

Years later, Jacob was about to see Esau for the first
time since he'd left home after cheating him of the
birthright. He sent men ahead to meet with Esau, and the
men returned, saying that Esau would come to meet him,
and had four hundred men with him. Jacob was naturally
fearful, and he went to great lengths to divide his men and
possessions into companies, in case Esau planned to
attack them. That night he sent his wives and children
away and was left alone. There, an angel came to Jacob,
and the two wrestled until daybreak. "When the man saw
that he did not prevail against Jacob, he struck him on the
hip socket; and Jacob's hip was put out of joint as he
wrestled with him" (Genesis 32:25). Jacob begged the
stranger to bless him, and finally the stranger did. When
Jacob asked his name, he said, "Why is it that you ask my
name?" Jacob realized that he had seen God face to face,
and he named the place Peniel. Jacob's meeting with Esau
shortly after that was one of reconciliation.

Jewish legend names this wrestling angel Camuel or Uriel, the Archangel. Another legend claims that the Archangel Raphael healed Jacob's hip joint. Some name the angelic wrestler Jacob-Israel, because the angel became a man.

Jael [Judaism]: tradition names Jael as one of the golden angels carved on the mercy seat of the Ark of the Covenant. The other angel was Zarall. One legend has these two angels facing one another when the Israelites were being faithful but having their faces turned from each other when they were out of fellowship with God.

Japhkiel [Judaism, Christianity]: according to some traditions, the angel who led the Israelites after they escaped from Egypt.

Jibril [Islam]: Arabic form of the name Gabriel, the Archangel.

Jesus [Christianity, Islam]: Angels appear at key moments in the life of Christ. The Archangel Gabriel foretold his birth to the Virgin Mary, who would become his mother (Luke 1). On the night of Christ's birth, angels announced his birth to shepherds who were working in the nearby fields (Luke 2). Angels instructed Mary and Joseph to flee to Egypt, lest King Herod kill the infant Jesus, then let them know when it was safe to return (Matthew 2). After Jesus' baptism, when he was led into the wilderness for a forty-day fast and was tempted by the devil, angels came afterward to take care of him (Matthew 4). The night before he was arrested and then put to death, an angel came to encourage Jesus while he agonized in prayer about the events to come (Luke 22). At his resurrection, angels appeared to the women who came to visit his tomb (Luke 24). And angels appeared when he later ascended into heaven, telling the onlookers that Jesus would return in the same way (Acts 1).

Likewise, when Jesus returns, he will be accompanied by angels. The apocalyptic vision of St. John, written as the book of Revelation, is filled with angels in various capacities, helping to carry out judgment and fight the final battle with Satan and his demons.

Jinn [Islam]: plural of jinni, or "genie." Islamic tradition categorizes angels as being created from light, whereas jinn were created from fire and humankind from clay. Even if jinn are considered angels, they are spirits of the lower, earthly realm—spirits that inhabit objects and places—and the term jinn is often used synonymously with demons. Another distinction some make between the jinn and angels is that angels do not have free will and thus cannot act against God's will, whereas jinn do have free will and sometimes use it malevolently.

According to Surah 38, God allowed King Solomon power over "the devils"; that term probably referred to jinn.

Joachim [Christianity]: Tradition names him as the father of Mary, the mother of Jesus. His wife Anne could not conceive, and an angel appeared to Joachim while he was away from home and told him to go back to his wife. After he returned home, Anne did conceive, and Mary was born.

Job, book of [Judaism, Christianity]: The story of the man Job reveals that Satan came to God and claimed that Job was righteous only because he had such a good life. God gave Satan permission to attack Job in any way he wanted, except that he could not kill Job. Thus began the saga of Job's troubles, which became a poetic exegesis of why bad things happen to good people.

John the Baptist [Christianity]: His birth was foretold by the Archangel Gabriel, who informed John's father, the priest Zechariah.

Jophiel [Christianity]: named in some traditions as one of the seven Archangels who stand before God. According to legend, it was Jophiel who drove Adam and Eve out of the Garden of Eden after they had sinned and who then stood guard so they could not re-enter.

Joseph [Christianity]: He was engaged to Mary when Gabriel visited the girl and foretold the miraculous birth of her son Jesus. Joseph did not believe that her pregnancy was divine and was about to quietly divorce her when an angel came to him in a dream and confirmed Mary's story, instructing Joseph to marry her (Matthew 1). After Jesus was born, Joseph was warned by an angel in another dream that Herod was out to kill the child and they must flee to Egypt (Matthew 2). And when it was safe to return home, an angel visited Joseph in another dream and told him so (Matthew 2).

Joshua [Judaism, Christianity]: He led the Israelites after the death of Moses. At Jericho, an angel appeared to Joshua with a drawn sword (Joshua 5:13–15). Joshua wanted to know if the angel was an Israelite or an adversary, and the angel replied, "Neither; but as commander of the army of the LORD I have now come." Tradition identifies this angel as the Archangel Michael.

Kabbalah [Judaism]: main tradition of mysticism and its writings, which have contributed much to Jewish angelology. Its primary text is the Zohar. Kabbalists devised systems for categorizing and naming angels and demons. Their use of incantations and formulas for conjuring spirits has historically crossed over into the practice of magic, which has never been encouraged by mainstream Jewish tradition or by rabbinic teaching.

Kaddishin [Judaism]: Along with the Irinim, they stand around God's throne and try the cases that come before God.

Karoz [Judaism]: In some lore, these are "reporter" angels who record the deeds of humans.

Ketzeph [Judaism]: in rabbinic lore, one of the five destroying angels, the angel of displeasure.

King of Angels [Judaism]: term sometimes used for the Archangel Metatron.

L

Lailah [Judaism]: angel of conception. The only angel of Jewish tradition that has female characteristics. She watches over the soul as it enters the semen and on through its formation, birth, and the soul's journey at death. Lailah represents nurture and motherhood, as opposed to Lilith, the she-demon who seeks to injure babies.

Last Judgment [Judaism, Christianity, Islam]: the event by which all mortals will be judged for their lives on earth and their manner of faith and righteousness. In all three of the Abrahamic traditions, angels are present at this judgment, accompanying souls to their judgment, presenting written records of each person, and taking souls to their final destination.

Latter-Day Saints [Christianity]: sect founded upon the teachings of Joseph Smith, who was said to have received special revelation from the angel Moroni, which became the Book of Mormon.

Legions [Judaism, Christianity]: military term reflecting a command of soldiers. This phrase has been used in describing the angels of heaven and also the demons of hell.

Lesser Yahweh [Judaism]: term sometimes used for the great angel Metatron. Yahweh signifies God's name; "lesser Yahweh" obviously marks Metatron as having authority second to God's.

Leviathan [Judaism]: a sea monster in Jewish lore; sometimes female and in some stories governs fallen angels.

Lie, angel of the [Christianity]: term used for Satan, because Satan is a great deceiver and liar.

Lilith [Judaism]: in some legends the first wife of Adam; she rebelled and became a major demon who sought to kill infants. The name given to female demons is Liliyot.

Lion's den [Judaism, Christianity]: where Daniel was thrown because he would not worship any god but the God of Israel. In the den, an angel came and closed the lions' mouths, and Daniel was saved (Daniel 6).

Lord, Angel of the [Judaism, Christianity]: term used for certain angels throughout Scripture who speak for God and at times appear to take on God's attributes and speak with more authority than angels in general.

Lot [Judaism, Christianity]: the nephew of Abraham who settled in Sodom with his wife and daughters. Three angels came to judge the city, and they warned Lot to take his family and flee. But he hesitated, so the angels took them by the hand and led them away before they destroyed Sodom and Gomorrah (Genesis 19).

Lucifer [Judaism, Christianity]: a great angel—the greatest according to some myths—who fell from heaven because he rebelled against God. Lucifer took other angels with him; these angels became demons in Christian belief. Lucifer is sometimes referred to as the Prince of Darkness and goes by other names such as Satan, Samael, or the devil.

Lumiel [Judaism]: In rabbinic lore this angel guards the entrance to the seventh and highest heaven.

Lying spirit [Judaism, Christianity]: In the book of 1 Kings, chapter 22, God, surrounded by all the heavenly host, asked, "Who will entice Ahab, so that he may go up and fall at Ramoth-gilead?" And God sent this angel to lie to the prophets of Ahab and thereby cause Ahab's death. God used an angel to deceive the wicked king. This is an instance of an angel's carrying out judgment. It is not clear whether this is an angel of God or a fallen angel (demon) put into God's service.

$$\mathcal{M}$$

Maggid [Judaism]: a spirit or angel who teaches the meaning of sacred texts; some Jewish mystics reportedly received instruction in this way.

Magic [Judaism, Christianity, Islam]: Angelology at times developed into magical and occult practices in Judaism and Islam; magical practice has traditionally been strictly forbidden in the Christian church, but certainly some witchcraft and satanic traditions developed out of Christianity as well, often using Christian sacraments and Scriptures perversely. Generally, rabbinic teaching has not supported occult practices, and traditional Sufi mysticism has not encouraged it. But religious beliefs about angels, coupled with the superstitions of folk religions, often resulted in magical practice. Human longing after power and secret knowledge have consistently fed the practices of magic and the occult (see Secret knowledge).

Malak [Islam]: Arabic word signifying angel. Malaika is the plural.

Malach [Judaism]: the Hebrew word for angel, which means messenger.

173

Malachi shalom [Judaism]: angels of peace. They protect worshipers after they leave the synagogue.

Malakim [Judaism]: another name for the order of angels known as Virtues.

Malik [Islam]: the angel put in charge of hell.

Manna [Judaism, Christianity]: the light, bread-like food sent from heaven to feed the Hebrews when they wandered in the wilderness. Manna is said to be the food of angels.

Manoah [Judaism, Christianity]: His wife was barren, and an angel of the Lord appeared to her and said that although she was barren, she would conceive and bear a son. The angel advised her against strong drink and unclean food. And her son was to be consecrated to God "from birth." This son would deliver Israel from the Philistines.

The woman—who, unfortunately, is not given a name—reports this incident to her husband, describing the visitor as a man who looks like an angel of God. Manoah prays that the angel will return and explain more about this supposed child-to-be. The angel does return, but again to the woman, not to Manoah, so the woman runs to get him. When they return, Manoah questions the visitor, who repeats, with a little more detail, what he told Manoah's wife. Manoah invites the visitor to eat with them; the man refuses the food for himself but suggests that they offer it as a sacrifice to the Lord. Manoah asks the man's name, to which he replies, "You must not ask for my name; it is unknowable!" (Tanakh). Manoah makes the burnt offering, and when the flames go up from the altar, the man ascends in them. At this, Manoah and his wife both fall to the ground in terror. The angel disappears, and Manoah is sure that they will both die now, because they have seen God. His wife doesn't agree; if God had wanted to kill them, why would he accept their offering and allow them to see and hear what they have just witnessed? The woman does give birth to a son, Samson, and God's spirit rests on him. (Judges 13)

Many-Eyed Ones [Judaism, Christianity]: term sometimes used for Cherubim. See this description in Revelation 4:8.

Mary, mother of Jesus [Christianity, Islam]: In the book of Luke, chapter 1, the girl engaged to Joseph is visited by Gabriel the Archangel. Gabriel announces that she, Mary, has found favor with God. She will become pregnant and give birth to a son, who will be called Son of the Most High. He will be given the throne of David, and his kingdom will never end. Mary is to name this boy Jesus. She innocently asks how this is possible, because she is still a virgin, and Gabriel tells her that the Holy Spirit will overshadow her. Not only that, Mary is informed, but also her barren cousin Elizabeth is six months pregnant at this very moment. Mary's response had become the Christian model of holy submission: She declares herself a servant of the Lord. "Let it be with me according to your word."

Mary Magdalene, [Christianity]: Jesus exorcised seven demons from her (Luke 8:2), and she became a close follower of his, even to the point of staying close by when he was crucified and going to the tomb later to anoint his body. She and another woman saw an angel at the tomb (Matthew 28:1–8).

Mastema [Judaism]: name used for the devil in the Book of Jubilees. According to some legends, this angel is the one given God's permission to test humans, and he did so with patriarchs such as Abraham and Moses.

Mawet [Judaism]: according to Jewish lore, the angel of death.

Melchizedek [Judaism, Christianity]: name of the priest and king of Salem to whom Abraham paid homage in Genesis 14. According to some legends, Melchizedek was also a very powerful angel who descended to earth to be an evangelist of sorts.

Mephistopheles: an angel often mistakenly thought to be named in Scripture but who appeared during the Renaissance in the legend of Faustus, a man who sold his soul to the devil. Mephistopheles is a term sometimes used to refer to the devil.

Merkabah, or merkavah [Judaism]: the chariot of the prophet's vision in Ezekiel 1. Out of this vision grew an entire branch of mysticism about people taking journeys to heaven and back while still alive. Angels that bore up the chariot are called Merkabah angels, and this term has also been applied to angels appearing in Merkabah legends in general.

Metatron [Judaism]: In Jewish legend, Metatron is the greatest of all the angels. Metatron was once the prophet Enoch, and when Enoch was translated to heaven, he was transformed into this mighty angel; God made a throne for him and gave him the name of Lesser Yahweh. Some legends say Metatron is the twin of Sandolphon, the angel who was, on earth, the prophet Elijah.

Michael [Judaism, Christianity, Islam]: one of the chief Archangels of Judaism and Christianity. He is the patron angel of the people of Israel and has been designated as the commander of heaven's armies (See Revelation chapters 12 and 20). According to some rabbinic writings, Michael serves as the high priest in heaven, mirroring the high priest in the Temple on earth. Like the other major Archangels Gabriel, Raphael, and Uriel, Michael has been connected with various legends and Scripture narratives, although he is named in only two or three of them.

In Islam, Michael is Mikha'il, one of the four Archangels. According to one legend, the Cherubim were created from the tears of Michael.

Michaelmas [Christianity]: feast day that honors Michael the Archangel. This was begun in the Eastern Orthodox Church but quickly became a celebration in Western Christendom as well. It is celebrated in the Eastern Orthodox Church on November 8 and in Western churches on September 29. In the Roman Catholic Church, this feast celebrates the three Archangels: Michael, Gabriel, and Raphael. In the Anglican Church it celebrates not only St. Michael the Archangel but all angels.

Middle Ages: sort of a golden era for angel lore and legend. Angels were depicted often in art and were assigned every possible function, from watching over specific hours of the day to making sure the planets themselves stayed their courses. Their names and legends multiplied, and there developed even more elaborate magic and mysticism surrounding them.

Mights [Christianity]: term sometimes used for the order of angels called Virtues.

Mika'il [Islam]: Arabic form of Michael, who is believed to watch over holy places and protect life in general.

Ministering spirits [Christianity]: angels, so named because one of their primary purposes is to minister to humankind according to God's plan and provision.

Miracles [Judaism, Christianity, Islam]: Angels are often assumed to be the source of miracles on earth. Scripture narratives give numerous accounts of angels overriding natural circumstances in order to bring a certain outcome. However, some theologians have claimed that angels do not override the order of nature or the elements but simply work within that created nature in ways that humans simply do not perceive. In other words, the "natural" order of God's created universe involves many principles and laws of which humans are ignorant and therefore unable to work with; the angels, having superior knowledge, can work within these principles, and when they do, they are certainly miracles from the standpoint of human beings.

The order of angels traditionally believed to perform miracles is the Virtues.

Morning Star [Christianity]: This phrase is applied to Jesus in Revelation 22:16, but in other mythology it has been used as a title for Lucifer.

Moroni [Christianity]: angel of the Mormons, said to have led Joseph Smith to the golden tablets on which was inscribed the Book of Mormon.

Moses [Judaism, Christianity, Islam]: chosen to lead the Hebrew slaves out of their bondage in Egypt. His story is found in the book of Exodus. Moses encountered angels several times. The first came in the form of a burning bush, out of which God spoke and commissioned Moses to be his people's leader. After the Israelites were released from Egypt and went on their journey to the land God had prepared for them, an angel resided with them in the form of a pillar of cloud by day and a pillar of fire by night.

In Exodus 23, God says, "I am sending an angel before you to guard you on the way and to bring you to the place that I have made ready. Pay heed to him and obey him. Do not defy him, for he will not pardon your offenses, since My Name is in him; but if you obey him and do all that I say, I will be an enemy to your enemies and a foe to your foes" (verses 20–22, Tanakh). The angel would go before the Israelites, through the lands of other tribes, whom God would wipe out.

After the Israelites sinned by creating and worshiping the golden calf, God once again assured them that his angel would go with them. However, at one point God declared to Moses, "But I will not go in your midst, since you are a stiffnecked people, lest I destroy you on the way" (Exodus 33:3, Tanakh). Evidently an angel would simply follow God's orders, while God might lose his temper. Moses pleaded with God to remain with them, and God relented.

Some legends claim that Michael the Archangel was the one that accompanied Moses, because Michael was the angel who argued with the devil over Moses' body after he died (Jude 9). Other legend makes Metatron the angel of the Exodus.

A prominent legend has Moses ascending into heaven when he went up to Mt. Sinai, and he encountered angels guarding the entrance and threatening to destroy him. But God allowed Moses in to give to him the Torah. There, Moses saw the great angel Sandalphon standing behind God's throne.

Muhammad, Prophet [Islam]: founder of Islam, who received the Qur'an as divine revelation from God, delivered by the Archangel Gabriel. Gabriel also took Muhammad on the Night Journey, where he went to Jerusalem and prayed with Jesus and other prophets and then was carried by Gabriel to heaven and back. Throughout his life, Muhammad received angelic assistance.

Munkar and Nakir [Islam]: the two angels who visit the tombs of people four days after death, questioning them and determining whether they will go to paradise or hell.

Music [Judaism, Christianity, Islam]: Some angels sing praise to God continually. All three faiths consider that divine music issues from the realms of heaven and is made by the angels or the cosmos in general. Angels have been depicted with harps and other musical instruments because of their association with heavenly music.

𝒩

Nakir and Munkar [Islam]: the two angels who visit the tombs of people days after their death, questioning them and determining whether they will go to paradise or hell.

Nations, angels of [Judaism, Christianity]: also called ethnarchs or archons, they are put in charge of individual nations, much as guardian angels are put in charge of individual people.

Nativity, angels of [Christianity]: Angels were present at the birth of Christ, announcing the event to shepherds in the nearby fields (Luke 2).

Nefilim [Judaism, Christianity]: giants mentioned in Genesis 4 that were the offspring of human women and a group of angels, called the Watchers in Jewish legend, who descended to earth.

Night Journey [Islam]: night on which the prophet Mohammad was accompanied by the angel Gabriel on a tour of the seven heavens, ending with Mohammad's encounter with God and some of the prophets.

Night of Power [Islam]: known as Laylat ul-Qadr, described in the Qur'an, Surah 97. On this night in 610 CE the angel Gabriel appeared to the Prophet Muhammad and gave to him the first revelation of sacred words that would become the Qur'an. This night began a period of revelation that lasted twenty-three years.

Noah [Judaism, Christianity]: patriarch who built the ark by which his family and two of every animal were saved when God sent the great Flood to wipe out evil humanity. One prominent Jewish legend has Noah building the ark according to instructions in a book that had been passed down through the generations since the angel Raziel gave it to Adam.

Nuriel [Judaism]: Legends name Nuriel as one of the tallest angels in heaven and one that met Moses when he made his journey through the seven heavens.

Ofanim [Judaism]: "Wheels," those angels upon which God's throne is carried. Similar to "Thrones" in the Christian hierarchy of angels.

Orders, angelic [Judaism, Christianity, Islam]: There are various hierarchies of angels listed in each tradition. The most standard in Christianity is that of Dionysius, later adopted by Thomas Aquinas. In Judaism, names of angel orders vary among rabbinic teachings and also within the mystical traditions. Islam gives no elaborate hierarchy of angelic orders; however there are several variations on them among the Sufi teachings.

Opposers of God [Judaism, Islam]: Some legends tell of opposition among the angels when God created humans and then when God showed them favor. In Judaism, Satan refused to show respect to human beings; in Islam, Iblis refused. In both cases, the angels were judged and punished because of this opposition.

Orifiel [Christianity]: listed by Pope Gregory as one of the seven Archangels.

Pargod [Judaism]: the curtain that separates God's throne from the angels and all the other heavenly realms. This is an obvious parallel to the curtain that separated the innermost chamber of the Temple in Jerusalem—the Holy of Holies—from the rest of the Temple space, where priests and the people were allowed.

Paul [Christianity]: apostle of Jesus and author of several letters to churches that became books of the New Testament. When the ship he was on was about to be overcome by a storm at sea, Paul encouraged the other men on the ship by saying that an angel had appeared to him and told him not to be afraid. The angel said that

Paul was destined to stand before Caesar, and God would keep safe all those who traveled with him (Acts 27). In 2 Corinthians 12, Paul makes reference to his journey to the third heaven. This reference is turned into a vivid and detailed story in the noncanonical *Apocalypse of Paul,* which describes Paul's tour of heaven and hell and his interaction with angel guides. Paul is sometimes thought to be the author of the epistle to the Hebrews, where it is said that angels are spirits whose work is to serve God's people (Hebrews 1:14).

Peace, Angel of [Judaism, Christianity]: another term for guardian angel, used in some Jewish apocalyptic literature and by some of the early Church Fathers and Mothers.

Penance, angel of [Judaism, Christianity]: traditionally thought to be the Archangel Phanuel. This angel is charged with correcting humans and moving them to penance and restoration.

Penial, or Penuel [Judaism]: Jacob wrestled with an angel at a place called Peniel. Some traditions named the angel Peniel.

Pestilence, angel of [Judaism, Christianity]: When King David took a census to assess his military power, God was angry for his lack of faith in God's protection. He gave David a choice of punishments: three years of famine, three months of devastation by Israel's foes, or three days of pestilence delivered by an angel of God. David counted on God's mercy and chose three days at the hand of the angel. So God sent an angel to spread pestilence through the land (1 Chronicles 21).

Peter [Christianity]: Peter was the apostle whom Jesus appointed to lead his church. When King Herod began persecuting the Christians, he threw Peter into prison. But during the night, an angel came to Peter, who was bound in chains between two guards. The angel "tapped Peter on the side and woke him, saying, 'Get up quickly.' And the chains fell off his wrists. The angel said to him, 'Fasten your belt and put on your sandals.' He did so. Then he said to him, 'Wrap your cloak around you and follow me.' Peter went out and followed him; he did not realize that what was happening with the angel's help was real; he thought he was seeing a vision. After they had passed the first and the second guard, they came before the iron gate leading into the city. It opened for them of its own accord and they went outside and walked along a lane, when suddenly the angel left him." (Acts 12:6–10).

Phanuel [Judaism, Christianity]: named by some sources as one of the four angels who stand in God's presence (the other three being Michael, Gabriel, and Raphael). According to early tradition in both Judaism and Christianity, Phanuel was the angel of penance, who inspired people to change their ways and turn to God.

Philip [Christianity]: He preached and worked wonders in the New Testament church. An angel instructed him to go on a certain road one day, and when he did so, Philip encountered a man reading from the book of Isaiah. The Holy Spirit urged Philip to go talk with the man, and he did so, and this resulted in the man's conversion and baptism (Acts 8).

Pillar of cloud, pillar of fire [Judaism, Christianity]: When the Israelites were freed from Egypt and journeyed to the place God had prepared for them, God sent an angel to stay with them. During the day the angel would be a pillar of cloud; at night it became a pillar of fire. The pillar would also rest at the tent of meeting whenever Moses met there with God. In Jewish lore, several different angels have been named as the specific angel who led the Israelites.

Pistis-Sophia [Judaism, Islam]: a feminine divine presence, sometimes referred to as an angel but often a personification of wisdom. Called Queen of Angels in the Gnostic tradition.

Prayers [Judaism, Christianity, Islam]: Jewish tradition and lore tell us that angels carry the prayers of righteous people to God. In Islamic tradition, angels are present in mosques when people pray, both listening to and recording their prayers. Christianity assumes that angels are witness to our prayers and are sometimes sent to help answer those prayers, particularly when people are in distress.

Preceptor angels [Judaism]: term for individual angels that became teachers and guides to the patriarchs.

Planets [Judaism, Christianity, Islam]: Angels have long been considered to be connected with astrology, and at various times specific angels were designated to be in charge of the planets. These lists vary according to source.

Potentates [Christianity]: a term sometimes used for the order of angels known as Powers.

Powers [Christianity]: the sixth order of angels in the hierarchy of Dionysius, third in the second triad.

Presence, angels of the [Judaism, Christianity]: those angels said to always be in God's presence. Some writings claim there are twelve of these. These angels could also be the seven Archangels mentioned in the Book of Tobit, who stand in God's presence. At least one Jewish tradition holds that there are four angels of the Presence: Michael, Gabriel, Uriel, and Penuel.

Prince of darkness [Judaism, Christianity]: title given to Satan in *The War of the Sons of Light Against the Sons of Darkness,* one of the writings contained in the Dead Sea Scrolls. This title has been used in general for the devil in various traditions.

Prince of God: sometimes refers to Michael the Archangel.

Prince of light [Judaism]: title given to the Archangel Michael in *The War of the Sons of Light Against the Sons of Darkness,* one of the writings contained in the Dead Sea Scrolls.

Prince of Persia [Judaism, Christianity]: In the tenth chapter of the book of Daniel, an angelic messenger says to Daniel, "Do not fear, Daniel, for from the first day that you set your mind to gain understanding and to humble yourself before your God, your words have been heard, and I have come because of your words. But the prince of the kingdom of Persia opposed me twenty-one days. So Michael, one of the chief princes, came to help me, and I left him there with the prince of the kingdom of Persia, and have come to help you . . ." From this passage developed the belief that certain regions of the world have their specific angel guardians, and that sometimes the angels struggle among themselves. We also have confirmation that some angels are "chief" in ranking.

Prince of the heavenly host [Judaism, Christianity]: one of the many titles for the Archangel Michael, because he has been identified as the leader of the heavenly armies.

Prince of the power of the air [Christianity]: title given to Satan in Ephesians 2:2 (KJV). Some translations read "ruler of the power of the air."

Prince of this world [Christianity]: in John's Gospel, Jesus used this term for Satan (12:31, KJV). Some translations use the word "ruler" instead of prince.

Principalities [Christianity]: the seventh order of angels in the hierarchy of Dionysius. They are believed to watch over nations and cities.

Pseudepigrapha [Judaism, Christianity]: writings excluded from the canon of Scriptures. Usually they are attributed to a great patriarch or apostle, but their authorship was questionable enough that the rabbis or church leaders did not accept their authority. These writings have been sources for much angel lore.

Psychepomp [Judaism]: an angel who guides the righteous to their final destination.

Putti [Christianity]: baby angels, also called cherubs. They have often appeared in apparitions of the Virgin, but there are no descriptions of angels in Scripture or the early traditions that are anything like the cute babies with wings that have become so prevalent in popular culture.

$\mathcal{Q}$

Queen of Heaven [Christianity]: title given to the Virgin Mary in 1954 by Pope Pius XII. Sometimes the term "Queen of Angels" is used interchangeably with Queen of Heaven.

Qumran [Judaism, Christianity]: site of several caves where many texts and fragments of texts were found in 1947. Among these were writings believed to come out of the Qumran community, called the Essenes, who practiced a very ritualized and ascetic religion within Judaism. Among the texts, known by the general name of the Dead Sea Scrolls, is *The War of the Sons of Light Against the Sons of Darkness* and *The Manual of Discipline,* both of which provide substantial material about angels. Also was found "The Angelic Liturgy," which is either a song cycle the angels themselves were purported to sing, or a special liturgy performed by priests in the hope of being transformed into angels.

Qur'an [Islam]: Islam's sacred book, its text revealed to the Prophet Mohammad by the Archangel Gabriel (Jibril). It contains more than a hundred references to angels. In the Qur'an, angels are represented as servants of God sent to bring revelation and help to humanity, as well as carry the dead to hell or paradise and participate on the Day of Judgment.

R

Radweriel [Judaism]: the angel who keeps the Book of Records. This book contains a record of all a person has said and done, and during the Jewish holy day of Rosh ha-Shanah, God can weigh the deeds and determine the person's destiny for the coming year.

Rahab [Judaism]: according to legend, angel or prince of the sea.

Raphael [Judaism, Christianity]: one of the chief Archangels. In the apocryphal book of Tobit, Raphael says to Tobit, "I am Raphael, one of the seven angels who stand ready and enter before the glory of the Lord" (Tobit 12:15). Raphael is considered the angel of healing in both Jewish and Christian lore. And he is one of the four primary Archangels that behold God's presence.

Raziel [Judaism]: known as the angel of secrets or the angel of magic in the kabbalistic tradition, Raziel was said to have written the book of Raziel, which contained secret knowledge, particularly astrology and divination. Raziel instructed Adam, or Noah, or both.

Raziel, book of [Judaism]: said to be written by the angel Raziel and given to Adam, presumably after Adam and

Eve were cast out of the Garden of Eden. This book contains secret knowledge about not only earth but also the heavenly realms, and includes much information about angels. Jewish legend has this book passed down through the line of Seth, although scholars place parts of its composition in the eleventh century.

Recording angels [Judaism, Islam]: Some angels record all the deeds of humankind. In Judaism, Radweriel keeps the Book of Records. In Islam, guardian angels (each person has two) also record the person's deeds. These records are opened and read on the Day of Judgment.

Resurrection [Christianity]: According to Matthew's Gospel, on the Sunday after the crucifixion of Jesus Christ, some of the women went to visit the tomb. An earthquake occurred, and an angel of the Lord came down, rolled the large stone from the tomb's entrance, sat on it, and spoke to the women: "Do not be afraid. I know that you are looking for Jesus who was crucified. He is not here; for he has been raised, as he said. Come, see the place where he lay. Then go quickly and tell his disciples, 'He has been raised from the dead, and indeed he is going ahead of you to Galilee; there you will see him.' This is my message for you."

Mark's account of this varies somewhat. The women arrive to find the stone already rolled away, and when they look inside the tomb, they see a young man in a white robe seated there, whose message is essentially the same as that in Matthew. And in Luke's account, the women find the tomb open, go inside, and then two men in brilliant clothes suddenly appear at their side. The men say, "Why do you look for the living among the dead? He is not here, but has risen."

In Judaism, Christianity, and Islam, angels will be present on the last day, when the righteous are resurrected.

Revelation, book of [Christianity]: the final book of the New Testament, which is a series of apocalyptic visions given to the apostle John while he was in exile on the island of Patmos. These visions reveal, through symbol and metaphor, the future of the church and of the final outcome in the battle between good and evil on earth. Angels figure prominently throughout this text. In *The Holy Angels,* Mother Alexandra identifies nineteen different functions of the angels in the book of Revelation, from the angels of the seven churches to the angel of the incense to the angel having the key to the bottomless pit.

Ridya [Judaism]: according to legend, angel or prince of rain.

Ridwan [Islam]: the angel put in charge of paradise.

Rigyon [Judaism]: River of fire in heaven, referred to in Daniel 7:10. It is said that certain angels are created out of this river each day, and they surround God's throne and sing praises all day, then go back to the river and are consumed. The next day, new angels are created from the river, and so on.

Ruh [Islam]: meaning "spirit," an angel that is much greater than all other angels, similar to the mythic proportions of Metatron in Jewish tradition.

Rulers [Christianity]: another term for the angelic order known generally as Powers. Rulers are listed in St. John of Damascus' hierarchy.

Ruman [Islam]: an angel said to subject the dead to trials and compel each person to write down his deeds.

Saints, and angels [Christianity]: Many legends and accounts of the saints include the visitation of, and help from, angels. It is difficult to distinguish between factual accounts and legends, but here is a sampling of saints associated with angels:

Agnes of Montepulciano
Ambrose
Angela of Foligno
Athanasius
Augustine
Bonaventure

Catherine of Siena
Clare of Montefalco
Frances of Rome
Francis de Sales
Francis of Assisi
Gregory Nazianzen
Gregory the Great
Jerome
John of Damascus
Patrick
Padre Pio
Rose of Viterbo
Teresa of Avila
Thomas Aquinas

Samael [Judaism]: another name for Satan. Samael has appeared in various legends.

Samriel [Judaism]: According to the Zohar, Samriel keeps the gates of hell. Before any soul enters, Samriel makes certain that person's name is in the Book of Gehenna.

Samson [Judaism, Christianity]: the son of Manoah, whose barren wife was finally blessed with a son. An angel appeared to her and also to Manoah, foretelling this event (Judges 13:1–18). Samson's supernatural strength made him a hero among the Israelites, but his weakness for the woman Delilah brought him to a tragic death.

Sandalphon [Judaism]: According to legend, the prophet Elijah became an angel when he was translated into heaven. As an angel his name is Sandalphon, and he is the twin of Metatron, the angel who was once the patriarch Enoch. It has been said that Sandalphon weaves garlands out of the prayers of Israel.

Sarah, wife of Abraham [Judaism, Christianity, Islam]: In Genesis 18, three angels visited her and Abraham one day and announced that the barren Sarah would conceive and give birth to a son. Sarah was in the tent and overheard this, and she laughed at the idea, because she and Abraham were both old. The angel speaking with Abraham heard her, and he asked if anything was too hard for God. He stated that, in one year, Sarah would indeed have a son. Sarah answered that she hadn't laughed, but the angel said, "Yes, you did laugh." The angel proved right; Sarah gave birth to a son, Isaac, just as predicted.

Sarim [Judaism]: meaning "Princes"; one of the higher angelic orders.

Satan [Judaism, Christianity, Islam]: the devil, adversary of humanity, the angel who rebelled against God and was cast out of heaven to become chief of the demons. Satan has several other names, such as Samael and Lucifer.

Secret knowledge [Judaism, Christianity, Islam]: Many prominent legends and Scripture narratives tell of angels' acting as interpreters or giving instruction to humans. The assumption is that some knowledge is too glorious, holy, or unfathomable to be entrusted to humans. Mystics in all three traditions have worked to enlighten themselves so that they could better understand such knowledge and wisdom. Those involved in occult practices have usually done so in order to obtain forbidden knowledge (and therefore power), often through relationship with angels, or in some cases demons. *The Book of Adam, The Book of Raziel,* and *The Testament of Solomon* are all examples of writings purported to be given to humans by angels in order to help humans master knowledge that was beyond them naturally.

Sennacherib [Judaism, Christianity]: king of the Assyrian army that came against the Israelites. An angel of the Lord destroyed the entire army—185,000 in one night (2 Kings 19:35).

Seraphim [Judaism, Christianity]: the first order of angels, nearest to God's throne; these angels sing praises continuously. The singular form is Seraph.

Seven Archangels [Judaism, Christianity]: Several traditions hold that seven Archangels stand before God's throne. The list of names varies, but the constants are Michael, Gabriel, Raphael, and Uriel.

Seven plagues [Christianity]: In the New Testament book of Revelation, seven angels appear in John's vision; each angel carries a plague. Later, each angel pours out a bowl, from which the plague is spilled upon the earth. (Chapters 15 and 16).

Seven stars, seven lampstands [Christianity]: In the New Testament book of Revelation, John's vision reveals seven stars and seven lampstands. It is revealed to John that the seven stars are the angels of the seven churches, and the seven lampstands represent the churches themselves.

Shayton [Islam]: Arabic form of "Satan"; can be used in the singular or plural, referring to Satan as chief of the jinn or to a group of fallen angels or demons.

Shekhinah [Judaism]: God's presence on earth, often considered the feminine representation of God or the bride of God. The Shekhinah is usually accompanied by angels. According to one legend, the angels mourned the departure of the Shekhinah after the destruction of the Temple.

Sheol [Judaism]: dwelling place of the dead.

Shepherds [Christianity]: Shepherds in Israel were on the low tier of society, but on the night Jesus was born, "an angel of the Lord stood before them, and the glory of the Lord shone around them, and they were terrified. But the angel said to them, 'Do not be afraid; for see—I am bringing you good news of great joy for all the people: to you is born this day in the city of David a Savior, who is the Messiah, the Lord. This will be a sign for you: you will find a child wrapped in bands of cloth and lying in a manger.' And suddenly there was with the angel a multitude of the heavenly host, praising God and saying, 'Glory to God in the highest heaven, and on earth peace among those whom he favors!'"(Luke 2:9–14).

Sijil [Islam]: according to the Qur'an (21:104), these angels take care of the scrolls in heaven until they are to be opened on the Day of Judgment.

Smith, Joseph [Christianity]: founder of Mormonism. In 1823, he was visited by the angel Moroni, who led him to where some golden tablets were buried and then helped Smith translate what was engraved on them. This became the Book of Mormon.

Sodom and Gomorrah [Judaism, Christianity]: These two cities were so wicked that God sent three angels to see if the wickedness was as terrible as had been reported. One of the angels agreed with Abraham that if even ten righteous people could be found in Sodom and Gomorrah, the cities would be spared God's wrath. Such righteousness could not be found, and the angels destroyed both cities.

Solomon, Testament of [Judaism]: a pseudepigraphical text, said to be penned by the great King Solomon. It gives an account of Solomon's dealing with demons during the building of the Temple. The book, which was probably written during the fourth century, serves as a catalogue of demons, their names, and their functions. Supposedly, Solomon received a magic ring from the Archangel Michael that enabled him to conjure the spirits and interrogate them.

Son of the morning [Judaism, Christianity]: name sometimes applied to Satan, or Lucifer.

Sons of Darkness [Judaism]: a term used for demons in the Dead Sea scrolls.

Sons of God [Judaism, Christianity]: traditional term for angels.

Sons of Light [Judaism]: a term used for angels in the Dead Sea scrolls.

Star: in various myths, angels are in charge of the stars or are otherwise related to them. Since earliest times "stars" has been a metaphor for angels, as mentioned in the books of Judges (5:20) and Job (38:7). Some ancient traditions held that very wise or righteous people would become angels. Such a transformation has been thought to be the reward of those people who made others wise.

Sufism [Islam]: esoteric and mystical branch of Islam. Much of the theory and lore about angels in Islam has come down from Sufi writers and teachers.

Tarshishim [Judaism]: in kabbalist hierarchies, an order of angels that would be similar to what Christian theologians later termed Virtues.

Teresa of Avila [Christianity]: mystic of the sixteenth century well known for her visions and writings. She once experienced an ecstasy in which an angel appeared with a spear and pierced her heart repeatedly. From her account: "I would see beside me, on my left hand, an angel in bodily form. . . . He appeared to be one of the highest types of angel who seem to be all afire. . . . In his hands I saw a long golden spear and at the end of the iron tip I seemed to see a point of fire. With this he seemed to pierce my heart several times. . . . The pain was so sharp that it made me utter several moans; and so excessive was the sweetness caused me by the intense pain that one can never wish to lose it, nor will one's soul be content with anything less than God."

Throne angels [Judaism, Christianity, Islam]: angels who bear up God's throne. In Judaism they are called, depending on the source, Arelim, Elohim, or Merkabah angels. In Christian tradition "Thrones" is a term for one of the nine choirs of angels, third in the hierarchy. In Islam, eight (or four, according to some sources) angels carry God's throne.

Thrones [Christianity]: the third order of angels in the hierarchy of Dionysius. They are said to bear up God's throne. They are described in Ezekiel 1 as having, or riding on, wheels, and so sometimes they have been called Wheels.

Tobit, book of [Judaism, Christianity]: In this story we meet the Archangel Raphael, who travels in disguise as a distant family member to help Tobias, son of Tobit. Raphael leads Tobias to Sarah and urges him to marry the woman. Because the demon Asmodeus has killed all seven of Sarah's former husbands, Raphael instructs Tobias in how to get rid of the demon. He also tells Tobias how to heal his father's blindness. Not surprisingly, Raphael is known as the angel of healing.

Torah, angel of the [Judaism]: One legend has the Israelites complaining because, while they are busy rebuilding the Temple, they don't have time to study the Torah. So God comes down and tells them how to invoke the Prince of the Torah, the angel who can teach them how to learn the Torah more quickly. The name of this angel is Yefefiah. Metatron has also been called Prince of the Torah.

Tree of Life [Judaism, Christianity]: After Adam and Eve ate of the Tree of Good and Evil, they had to be kept from the Tree of Life, so that they would not live forever. God sent the two from the Garden, and he placed two Cherubim to guard the Tree of Life.

In Kabbalist mysticism, the tree of life becomes a diagram of God's attributes, and sometimes an Archangel is associated with each branch.

Trisagion [Judaism, Christianity]: Based upon Isaiah 6:3 and Revelation 4:8 is the belief that this prayer is sung constantly to God by the angels; most likely those in the angelic choir closest to God's presence: the seraphim, cherubim, and throne angels. They circle God's throne and sing:

"Holy, holy, holy is Yahweh Sabaoth.
His glory fills the whole earth" (Isaiah 6:3, Tanakh).
or
"Holy, holy, holy
is the Lord God, the Almighty,
who was and is and is to come" (Revelation 4:8).

The Orthodox Church uses the prayer: "Holy God, Holy Mighty, Holy Immortal, have mercy on us." The Orthodox believe that this hymn was divinely revealed in Constantinople.

Trumpets [Judaism, Christianity, Islam]: often associated with angels. Jesus said that at the sound of the trumpet his second coming would occur. In the book of Revelation, seven angels blow seven trumpets, each announcing an event of the apocalypse. The Archangel Gabriel will sound the trumpet of the Last Judgment.

Tutelary angels [Judaism, Christianity]: a term for angels that guard specific nations. They are also called archons, ethnarchs, and princes.

Tzadkiel [Judaism]: Depending on the source, this angel is one of the seven Archangels, is one of the two Sabbath angels that accompany a man home on the Sabbath (Tzadkiel is the good angel of this pair), was the teacher of Abraham, or dresses souls in new garments when they enter paradise.

U

Unclean spirits [Judaism, Christianity]: term applied to evil spirits, or demons.

Uriel [Judaism, Christianity]: Tradition names Uriel as one of the chief Archangels and one of the four angels of the Presence. The mythology surrounding this angel is profuse; some Jewish legends identify Uriel as the angel that wrestled with Jacob. He has also been identified as the angel set as a guard over the Garden of Eden after Adam and Eve were sent away, the angel who warned

Noah about the coming deluge, and the one who guarded the tomb where Jesus was buried and who announced his resurrection to the disciples on the road to Emmaus. Some sources place Uriel in charge of hell. And in the apocryphal book of 2 Esdras, Uriel is named as the angel who serves as interpreter and teacher to the prophet Ezra. Uriel's name means "God is my light"; in Jewish tradition he is considered the angel that lights our way.

$\mathscr{V}$

Valkyrie: an early Nordic version of angels. They were female and came to battlefields to accompany fallen warriors to the hereafter.

Vengeance, angels of [Judaism, Christianity, Islam]: in the same general category as angels of destruction, because they carry out God's judgment upon sinners. It is generally assumed that these are not evil or fallen angels but simply angels carrying out God's judgment.

Victor [Christianity]: Irish legend claims the man that came to St. Patrick in a dream, telling him to return to Ireland, was actually an angel named either Victor or Victorious.

Virgin Mary [Christianity, Islam]: She gave birth to Jesus. Catholic tradition claims that she did not die but was assumed into heaven and was crowned Queen of Heaven. She is considered Queen of the Angels. In various apparitions of the Virgin, she has been accompanied by angels, often cherubs.

Virtues [Judaism, Christianity]: the fifth order of angels according to Dionysius. This places them in the second triad of the heavenly hierarchy, that group of angels between the first triad, which attends only to God, and the third, which deals with earthly matters. Angels of this second triad have been credited with running the natural universe, and they are responsible for miracles, or at least phenomena that humans perceive as miracles. According to Gustav Davidson, they are the equivalent of Malakim or Tarshishim in Hebrew tradition.

W

War in heaven [Christianity]: As described in Revelation 12:7–9: "And war broke out in heaven; Michael and his angels fought against the dragon. The dragon and his angels fought back, but they were defeated, and there was no longer any place for them in heaven. The great dragon was thrown down, that ancient serpent, who is called the Devil and Satan, the deceiver of the whole world—he was thrown down to the earth, and his angels were thrown down with him."

Watchers [Judaism, Christianity]: Several versions of this legend exist. The Watchers were a high order of angels, named thus because they never slept. According to one source, two hundred Watchers descended from heaven to dwell on earth among people. Although they intended simply to help the humans, they became sexually attracted to the women and soon were cohabiting with them, which resulted in the Nefilim, or giants, mentioned in Genesis 6. The Watchers also taught humans magic as well as secrets of the natural universe that God did not intend for humans to know. And these fallen angels became ravenous in every way, eating all manner of beasts and having sex with not only women but men and animals.

In Christian tradition, the Watchers were named Grigori. They were considered the lowest form of angel, which would explain their bodily form and ability to reproduce with human women. But according to some versions of the Jewish legend, they were a high order of angel until they chose to come to earth (some stories say that two came; others give the number as two hundred), and when they descended their form changed from one of heavenly splendor to that of earthly beings. The leaders of the Watchers, Shemhazai and Azazel, are subjects of other legends.

In the vision recounted in Daniel 4:13, we find the term "holy watcher," which probably applied to an angel in the vision.

Wheels [Judaism, Christianity]: the "many-eyed ones" of Ezekiel 1. In Jewish tradition they have been identified as

Arelim, Elohim, or Merkabah angels. They are also known as Thrones in Christian tradition, because they bear up God's throne in heaven.

Winds: Hebrews 1:7 says, "He makes his angels winds, / and his servants flames of fire." Revelation 7:1 refers to four angels holding back the four winds of the earth. Numerous angels have been identified in legend as being guardians of the four winds.

Wings: Many traditions the world over give wings to their spirit messengers. This was true in Babylon, where the Jews were in exile, and it's likely that Jewish lore adopted some of these images. Greek and Roman gods, such as Hermes and Eros, also had wings. In the Hebrew Bible, certain angels are described having wings, namely, the Seraphim and Cherubim. The Qur'an describes angels with wings in Surah 35. The fact that angels come and go so easily and are often seen in the heavens implies some power of flight. However, wings themselves (which did not become part of Christian angel lore until the time of Constantine) serve primarily as symbols of the angels' ability to go wherever God sends them.

Wormwood [Christianity]: The name of a star in Revelation 8 that falls from heaven and onto a third of the earth's rivers and springs, making them bitter to the point of causing death in those that drink from them. Wormwood has been identified as Satan or as a demon.

Yazriel [Judaism]: According to one legend, this angel guards the shard of the Foundation Stone, on which God's names are written. The angel has tools, and as quickly as humanity's sin wipes out a name of God, the angel Yazriel carves it anew.

Yefefiah [Judaism]: according to legend, the angel who taught Moses the secret to learning the Torah. Yefefiah is sometimes referred to as the Prince of the Torah or Angel of the Torah.

Yurkemi [Judaism]: in some legends prince of the hail, or angel in charge of hail.

Zabaniya [Islam]: According to some writings, zabaniya are special angels who tend to the damned in hell.

Zachariel [Christianity]: named as the seventh Archangel by Saint Gregory the Great.

Zadkiel [Judaism, Christianity]: named as the seventh Archangel by Psuedo-Dionysius. (See Tzadkiel).

According to one legend, Zadkiel prevented Abraham from sacrificing his son Isaac.

Zarall [Judaism]: Tradition names Zarall as one of the golden angels carved on the mercy seat of the Ark of the Covenant. The other angel was Jael. One legend has these two angels facing one another when the Israelites were being faithful but having their faces turned from each other when the people were out of fellowship with God.

Zechariah [Christianity, Islam]: The same angel Gabriel who appeared to Mary, announcing her coming pregnancy, appeared earlier in the sanctuary beside the altar, when Zechariah the priest was serving. Gabriel announced that Zechariah's barren and elderly wife, Elizabeth, would give birth to a son, who would be filled with the Holy Spirit from the womb and would turn many of the children of Israel back to God. Zechariah questioned how this was possible. His question was much in the same vein as Mary's when Gabriel announced a similar message to her. But, possibly because Zechariah was a priest, well versed in Scripture and in God's history with the Israelites, Gabriel had little patience with him, replying, "I am Gabriel. I stand in the presence of God, and I have been sent to speak to you and to bring you this good news. But now, because you did not believe my words, which will be fulfilled in their time, you will become mute, unable to speak, until the day these things occur" (Luke 2:19-20). Zechariah remained mute until the birth of his son, who became John the Baptist.

Zechariah, book of [Judaism, Christianity]: Dated 520 BCE, this prophetic book was probably written by a man named Zechariah as well as other authors. The first eight chapters contain visions in which angels both act and interpret what is happening. In chapter 1 is the man "standing among the myrtle trees"; in chapter 2 another angel appears as a "man with a measuring line in his hand"; in chapter 3 the prophet is shown "the high priest Joshua standing before the angel of the Lord, and Satan standing at his right hand to accuse him" and hears the exchange among the three. In the following several visions, the angel companion is there to explain what the visions mean.

Zodiac, angels of: Since Medieval times, astrology has been intertwined with angelology. At times, a person's star was associated with his or her deputy angel. And there have been various lists of angels said to be in charge of the zodiac signs. Not only do the lists vary from source to source, but also in some systems they shifted with the seasons of the year.

Zohar [Judaism]: the major text of kabbalist mysticism. It is attributed to Shimon ben Yohai, a rabbi of the second century, but is more likely the work of a Spanish writer of the thirteenth century, Moses de Leon, who claimed to have discovered and published the earlier rabbi's works. It is a commentary on the Pentateuch containing secret information (taught by God to certain angels who then taught certain spiritual men such as Moses); this learning was passed on orally through the patriarchs until it was written down by the rabbi. The Zohar remains a primary source for mysticism of Kabbalah.

Angel Prayers

Angel of God, my guardian dear,
To whom God's love entrusts me here,
Ever this day be at my side,
To light and guard, to rule and guide.
—traditional Catholic prayer to a guardian angel

Angel of God, my holy guardian, given me by God to
protect me, I pray thee earnestly; enlighten me this day;
from all harm shield me; toward good advise me; and on
the path of salvation guide me.
—Orthodox Lauds

May the fasting break their fast in your home, and may
the dutiful and pious eat your food, and may the angels
send prayers upon you.
—Islam, prayer for breaking a fast

O most holy Angel of God, appointed by Him to be my
guardian, I give you thanks for all the benefits which
you have bestowed on me in body and in soul. I praise
and glorify you that you did condescend to assist me
with such patient fidelity, and to defend me against all
the assaults of my enemies. Blessed be the hour in which
you were assigned to me as my guardian,
my defender, and my patron.
—St. Gertrude

Angel, little angel mine, given me by God: I am small,
you make me big, I am weak, you make me strong.
—Orthodox children's prayer

We who mystically represent the Cherubim, and sing to
the life-giving Trinity the thrice-holy hymn, let us now
lay aside all earthly cares that we may receive the King
of Glory like a Conqueror upon a shield and spears, by
His Angelic Hosts invisibly upborne,
Alleluia, Alleluia, Alleluia.
—Cherubic Hymn (Orthodox)

St. Michael the archangel, defend us in battle, be our
protector against the malice and snares of the devil. We
humbly beseech God to command him, and do thou, O
Prince of the heavenly host, by the divine power thrust
into hell Satan and the other evil spirits
who roam about the world seeking the ruin of souls.
—early Roman liturgy

Saint Michael,
first champion of the Kingship of Christ, pray for us.
—Pope Pius XI

O God, who did give blessed Raphael the Archangel to
Thy servant Tobias, as a companion on his journey:
grant to us, Thy servants, that we may always be guarded
by his care and strengthened by his help.
—Feast of St. Raphael, Tridentine Roman Missal

O thou who speedest through all space
More swiftly than the lightnings fly,
Go very often in my place
to those I love most tenderly.
With thy soft touch, Oh, dry their tears,
Tell them the Cross is sweet to bear,
Speak my name softly in their ears,
And Jesus' Name supremely fair!
—St. Thérèse of Lisieux

We humbly beseech Thee, Almighty God, command
these [consecrated bread and wine] to be carried by the
hands of Thy holy Angel to thine Altar on High.
—Roman liturgy

God our Father, in a wonderful way You guide the work
of angels and men. May those who serve You constantly
in heaven keep our lives safe from all harm here on
earth. Grant this through our Lord Jesus Christ, your
Son, who lives and reigns with You and the Holy Spirit,
one God, for ever and ever. Amen
—Feast of the Holy Archangels, Michael, Gabriel and
Raphael, Roman Missal

May the offering of our service, O Lord, and the prayer
of the blessed Archangel Gabriel be acceptable in Thy
sight, O Lord; that he whom we venerate on earth, may
be our advocate before Thee in heaven. Through Christ
our Lord. Amen.
—Tridentine Roman Missal

By the intercession of blessed Michael the Archangel,
standing at the right hand of the altar of incense, and of
all his elect, may the Lord vouchsafe to bless this
incense, and receive it as an odor of sweetness.
—Roman liturgy

O Master, Lord our God, who has appointed in Heaven Orders and Hosts of Angels and Archangels for the service of Thy glory; cause that our entrance there may be an entrance of Holy Angels serving with us and glorifying Thy greatness for unto Thee are due all glory, honor and worship to the Father, and to the Son, and to the Holy Ghost: now and ever and unto ages of ages. Amen.
—Orthodox liturgy

O holy Angel
who didst strengthen Jesus Christ our Lord,
come and strengthen us also; come and tarry not.
—Pope Pius X

O glorious Prince of the heavenly host, Saint Michael the Archangel, defend us in the battle and in the fearful warfare that we are waging against the principalities and powers, against the rulers of this world of darkness, against the evil spirits. Come thou to the assistance of men, whom Almighty God created immortal, making them in His own image and likeness and redeeming them at a great price from the tyranny of Satan. Fight this day the battle of the Lord with the legions of holy Angels, even as of old thou didst fight against Lucifer, the leader of the proud spirits and all his rebel angels, who were powerless to stand against thee, neither was their place found any more in heaven. . . . Changing himself into an

angel of light, he goes about with the whole multitude of the wicked spirits to invade the earth and blot out the Name of God and of His Christ, to plunder, to slay and to consign to eternal damnation the souls that have been destined for a crown of everlasting life. . . . These crafty enemies of mankind have filled to overflowing with gall and wormwood the Church, which is the Bride of the Lamb without spot; they have laid profane hands upon her most sacred treasures. Make haste, therefore, O invincible prince, to help the people of God against the inroads of the lost spirits and grant us the victory. Amen.
—Pope Leo XIII

O Holy Angel, that keepest guard over my despondent soul and passionate life, leave me not a sinner nor depart from me.
—Orthodox prayer to guardian angel

Peace unto you, O ministering angels.
—Jewish blessing

May the angel who redeems from all harm bless the children.
—Jewish bedtime prayer

Praise the LORD from the heavens;
praise Him on high.
Praise Him, all His angels,
praise Him, all His hosts.
—Psalm 148:1, Tanakh

ACKNOWLEDGMENTS

Many thanks to Lil Copan, Warren Farha, Dr. Laleh Bakhtiar, and Rabbi Aaron Spiegel for their invaluable help on this blessed yet complex and many-layered topic.

SELECTED SOURCES

Barnstone, Willis, ed. *The Other Bible: Ancient Alternative Scriptures.* San Francisco: HarperSanFrancisco, 1984.

Cross, F.L., and E.A. Livingstone, eds. *The Oxford Dictionary of the Christian Church.*

Danielou, Jean. *The Angels and their Mission According to the Fathers of the Church.* Allen, Tex.: Thomas More Publishing, 1957.

Davidson, Gustav. *A Dictionary of Angels.* New York: The Free Press, 1967.

Farah, Caesar E. *Islam: Beliefs and Observances.* Barron's Educational Series, Inc., 1994.

Giudici, Maria Pia. *The Angels: Spiritual and Exegetical Notes.* New York: Alba House, 1993.

Glassé, Cyril. *The New Encyclopedia of Islam.* New York: Rowman & Littlefield Publishers, 2001.

Godwin, Malcolm. *Angels: An Endangered Species.* New York: Barnes & Noble Books, 2001.

Gordon, Matthew S. *Islam: Origins, practices, holy texts, sacred persons, sacred places.* New York: Oxford University Press, 2002.

Kreeft, Peter. *Angels (and Demons): What Do We Really Know about Them?* San Francisco: Ignatius Press, 1995.

Maqsood, Ruqaiyyah Waris. *Teach Yourself Islam*. Chicago: McGraw-Hill, 2003.

Metford, J.C.J. *Dictionary of Christian Lore and Legend*. London: Thames and Hudson, 1983.

Mother Alexandria: *The Holy Angels*. Minneapolis, Minn.: Light and Life Publishing Company, 1987.

Nasr, Seyyed Hossein. *An Introduction to Islamic Cosmological Doctrines*. New York: State University of New York Press, 1993.

Nasr, Seyyed Hossein, ed. *Islamic Spirituality: Foundations*. New York: Crossroad, 1991.

Neusner, Jacob, and Alan J. Avery-Peck. *The Blackwell Companion to Judaism*. Malden, Mass.: Blackwell Publishing, 2003.

Peters, F.E. *Judaism, Christianity, and Islam: The Classical Texts and Their Interpretation. Vol. 3: The Works of the Spirit*. Princeton, N.J.: Princeton University Press, 1990.

Pickthall, Mohammed Marmaduke. *The Meaning of the Glorious Koran: An explanatory translation*. Chicago: Kazi Publications, n.d.

Renard, John. *Seven Doors to Islam: Spirituality and the Religious Life of Muslims*. Berkeley, Calif.: University of California Press, 1996.

Russell, Jeffrey Burton. *A History of Heaven: The Singing Silence*. Princeton, N.J.: Princeton University Press, 1997.

Schwartz, Howard. *Tree of Souls: The Mythology of Judaism.* New York: Oxford University Press, 2004.

Segal, Alan F. *Life after Death: A History of the Afterlife in Western Religion.* New York: Doubleday, 2004.

Staniloae, Dumitru. *The Experience of God: Orthodox Dogmatic Theology. Volume Two: The World: Creation and Deification.* Brookline, Mass.: Holy Cross Orthodox Press, 2000.

Trachtenberg, Joshua. *Jewish Magic and Superstition: A Study in Folk Religion.* Philadelphia: University of Pennsylvania Press, 2004.

Voragine, Jacobus de. *The Golden Legend.* New York: Penguin Books, 1998.

Waines, David. *An Introduction to Islam.* Cambridge University Press, 1995.

Zepp, Ira G., Jr. *A Muslim Primer: Beginner's Guide to Islam.* 2nd ed. Fayetteville: The University of Arkansas Press, 2000.